BRIDGING THE CULTURE GAP

A PRACTICAL GUIDE TO INTERNATIONAL BUSINESS COMMUNICATION

2nd edition

PENNY CARTÉ AND CHRIS FOX

Canning

**KOGAN
PAGE**

London and Philadelphia

First published in Great Britain and the United States in 2004 by Kogan Page Limited
Second edition 2008
Reprinted 2008, 2009

Kogan Page Limited
120 Pentonville Road
London N1 9JN
United Kingdom
www.koganpage.com

Kogan Page US
525 South 4th Street, #241
Philadelphia PA 19147
USA

© Penny Carté and Chris Fox, 2004, 2008

The right of Penny Carté and Chris Fox to be identified as the authors of this work has been asserted by them in accordance with the Copyright, Designs and Patents Act 1988.

ISBN 978 0 7494 5274 2

British Library Cataloguing-in-Publication Data

A CIP record for this book is available from the British Library.

Library of Congress Cataloging-in-Publication Data

Carté, Penny.
   Bridging the culture gap : a practical guide to international business communication
Penny Carté & Chris Fox. -- 2nd ed.
      p. cn.
   Includes bibliographical references and index.
   ISBN 978-0-7494-5274-2
   1. Business etiquette. 2. Intercultural communication. 3. Business communication.
4. National characteristics. I. Fox, Chris J., 1973- II. Title.
   HF5389.C36 2008
   395.5'2--dc22
                                                                        2008011169

Typeset by Jean Cussons Typesetting, Diss, Norfolk
Printed and bound in Great Britain by MPG Books Ltd, Bodmin, Cornwall

Contents

About Canning   *vii*
About the authors   *ix*
Foreword   *xi*
Acknowledgements   *xiii*

Introduction   1

1 **Interpreting the party line**   5
*The harder the global organization tries to present a united
front, the greater the scope for conflict and misunderstanding.
How can you bridge the gap between HQ and subsidiary?*
Mission statements 6; Corporate initiatives 8; Working
rhythms 14; Communication styles 17

2 **Knowing your place**   21
*On home ground, an employee usually knows where others fit
into the hierarchy, and how they expect to be treated.
Abroad, however, it's easy to upset people without realizing it.
How can you make sure you're speaking to the right person
in the right way?*
Handling the hierarchy 23; Taking responsibility 30;
Monitoring performance 32; Getting people to play ball 36

3 Knowing the limits   45

*In their own culture, most people will have a pretty good idea
of what they should or shouldn't do. But, how well do your
notions of right and wrong travel?*

Rules, regulations and the laws of the land 47; Gifts, favours
and bribes 52; Nepotism 56; Discretion versus dishonesty 60

4 Knowing the form   65

*Good manners are valued by every culture. But how
international are the social behaviours you learnt at your
mother's knee?*

Greeting people 67; Making small talk 70; Playing the
conversation game 71; Choosing what to say and how to
say it 73; Trying to be funny 78; Avoiding hidden dangers 81

5 Making presentations   85

*Companies today spend millions on training their managers
to make more effective presentations. But will the techniques
you learnt at home be equally effective when you go abroad?*

Choosing the right style 87; Finding a concrete context 97;
Speaking with impact 103

6 Making deals   111

*The success of any deal depends as much on the strength
of the relationship as on the clauses in the contract. But
negotiating styles vary considerably from culture to culture.
What adjustments do you need to make when you're
negotiating in the international arena?*

Picking the right people 113; Thinking about pace and
place 118; Playing the game to win 123

7 Making yourself understood in English   137

*Whatever your nationality or native tongue, you will probably
use English to communicate with your international
counterparts. But their version of English will be different
from yours. How can you learn to speak Offshore English
which is the true lingua franca of international commerce?*

Language 139; Communication techniques 150

8 Knowing yourself   **161**

Knowing yourself is the first step to knowing others.
Where do you fall on the cultural preference scales? And
how should you adapt your approach when you meet
someone who is at the opposite end of the scale from you?
Relationships 163; Communication 169; Time 172;
Truth 176; The meaning of life 179; Presentation style 181;
A final word 183

Appendix: False friends   **185**
A list of words whose meanings may be misunderstood

References   *191*
Further reading   *193*
Index   *197*

Praise for *Bridging the Culture Gap*

"Amazing how much practical value one can take from this book on the complex topic of communicating across culture. Clear proof that Canning can communicate sophisticated topics in a crisp, entertaining and highly meaningful way. The busy reader gets the key points on the fly – ideal in-flight reading."
Dr Siegfried Schuetzinger, Head of PB Training, *PBST, F. Hoffmann-La Roche*

"To work with Canning is to go on a stimulating journey. Their team of consultants has a wide range of cross-cultural experience. Their method is to make you learn by doing. Their debriefing sessions focus on business efficiency and are seasoned with just the right amount of British humour. Since the very beginning of the Alliance between Renault and Nissan, our partnership with Canning has contributed greatly to the success of our joint work."
Philippe Millon, Executive staff development and training, *Renault*

"Canning offers tough and intensive training, but brilliant results. I believe this book will do the same thing for anyone looking for success in cross-cultural business."
Takashi Kashiwagi, Corporate Officer, Head of Sales, *sanofi-aventis KK.*

"As an American who worked in Europe for three years in the early 2000s, and now working in Texas, I find *Bridging the Culture Gap* to be a practical guide for communicating and influencing across cultures. The authors use authentic and engaging anecdotes, which will help readers to understand their own culture, and others' reactions to it in the context of everyday business."
Gary Kuusisto, Training Manager, *Thomas Petroleum*

"Full of real-life examples and practical advice which reflects the experience and skills of its masterful but unpretentious authors."
Andreas Molck-Ude, Head of Africa and Middle East Division, *Munich Re*

About Canning

Canning is a UK-based company whose expertise lies in communication. We help business and professional people from all over the world to communicate effectively with each other across linguistic and cultural barriers. Canning's 51 trainers and consultants have run courses at our centres in the United Kingdom, Italy and Japan and in another 53 countries on five continents. Over 130,000 people have attended these courses since 1965.

Canning was one of the first training companies to offer specialist cross-cultural skills programmes, tailored for business. The training consultants who have contributed real-life stories to this book are, for the most part, members of our cross-cultural skills team. Together they have first-hand experience of working in a variety of fields in almost every country in Europe, as well as further afield in Africa, Asia, North America, South America and Australasia.

Since 2000, for example, we have helped over 3,400 Renault and Nissan employees in Europe, the United States, Thailand and Japan to bridge the cultural gap in their Alliance. Hoffmann-La Roche is also a major user of our international teambuilding, facilitation and cross-cultural skills services – we have worked with over 350 of their people in the past 3 years. And since 2005, we have been helping managers at Air France and KLM to build efficient, multicultural, cross-company teams. So far, we have run programmes for over 1,100 of their managers in 27 different countries.

Other current and regular cross-cultural skills clients include the Bank for International Settlements, BT Global Services, Capgemini, Lloyds Register of Shipping, Munich Re., Nortel, Panasonic, Quintiles, Samsung, Schneider Electric, the Stockholm School of Economics, Technip and Valeo.

Among the other communication skills courses that we run around the world are: *Presenting Effectively, Writing Clearly and Powerfully, and Negotiating Successful International Deals.*

About the authors

Penny Carté is a modern languages graduate who has lived and worked in France, Italy and Japan. During her 31 years with Canning she has run tailored courses for multinational companies from the automotive, pharmaceutical, chemical and financial sectors, and has travelled extensively throughout Europe and Asia. She now specializes in one-to-one coaching, helping senior managers to prepare for specific projects. Since 1988, she has also written and edited a wide range of cross-cultural, management skills and English for Business training materials.

Chris Fox is a politics graduate. He spent six months as a radio broadcaster in Belgrade during the Balkan conflict before taking up a position at the University of Reading, where he taught political and cultural theory. He then went on to work as a researcher and negotiator within a trade union before joining Canning in 1999. He specializes in running media, presentation and negotiation skills seminars across a wide range of sectors, as well as acting as Key Account Manager to some of Canning's biggest clients, and overseeing Canning's marketing activities.

The production of this book was very much a team effort. While Penny Carté and Chris Fox developed the format and wrote the actual text, much of the knowledge and experience it distils came from Canning's team of international cross-cultural consultants. It is only right, therefore, that the names of the most prolific contributors should also appear on this page:

Richard Pooley is Canning's Managing Director. During his 30 years with the company, he has pioneered and run a range of skills and cross-cultural programmes, managed Canning's Tokyo subsidiary and led his own multi-cultural team. The author of many articles on cross-cultural skills, he frequently speaks at international conferences.

Nigel White heads Canning's International Training & Development division. With Canning since 1986, he spent his first nine years in Tokyo. A negotiation and cross-cultural skills specialist, and the author of two books, he divides his time between training, selling and consulting in Asia, Europe and Japan.

Gerard Bannon started his Canning career in 1989 with a four-year appointment in Tokyo. Now a Senior Consultant in the UK team, he is responsible for Canning's generic cross-cultural skills courses. He also project manages the 'Optimizing our Teamwork' programme that Canning runs, all over the world, for a large international client.

Foreword

Anticipating and understanding cultural differences and being able to adapt the way you communicate accordingly is the foundation of any successful international business. Reinsurance – the business I am in – is, by its very nature, global. If we want to be successful, we have to be able to do business in diverse cultural and linguistic environments. What may work perfectly well in, say, Norway can lead to disaster in Japan.

That's why, in 2002, we decided to run an in-depth negotiation training programme for the members of our Middle Eastern and African business units. The search for a training provider brought me into contact with Canning, who were already a long-standing partner of ours in the field of negotiation training, and Chris Fox helped us put together an expanded programme, including on-going coaching.

The training quickly dispelled the myths that surround international negotiations. Indeed, those of us who were looking to learn magic tricks for instant negotiating success were initially disappointed by the seemingly unspectacular observations and conclusions we were confronted with. But we were soon flabbergasted to discover that, in practice, they made a real difference to our negotiating ability. Most notably, we realized the huge, and often underestimated, impact that language and grammar can have on the results of negotiations. Subsequently, Canning customized the training to the individual teams, who, though they considered it tough, were spurred on by measurable progress in their results. Although it was originally a management idea, the members of the teams now insist on getting this negotiation coaching regularly.

This book is a practical, easy-to-read guide for international business people who, like my team members and me, are seeking to adapt their communication skills to the international arena. It will help them within their own organizations, and when dealing with international clients or suppliers. It raises awareness of cross-cultural differences, and serves as a reference for those who wish to refresh their memory of specific DOs and DON'Ts. Most of all, it is full of real-life examples and practical advice which reflect the experience and skills of its masterful but unpretentious authors.

Andreas Molck-Ude
Head of Africa and Middle East Division
Munich Re

Acknowledgements

The cultural preference scales that appear in this book were developed by Canning and have been refined, over the past 14 years, with the help of our international course participants. We acknowledge, however, that the thinking behind them and some of the terminology we have used was originally inspired by the research and theories of Edward T Hall – high versus low context communication styles, polychronic versus monochronic time systems; Geert Hofstede – individualist versus collectivist (ie group-oriented) societies; and Fons Trompenaars – achievement versus ascription (ie achieved versus given status), universalism versus particularism (ie fixed versus relative truth). These three experts have contributed so much to the international debate on differing cultural behaviours that their influence is bound to be reflected in any serious examination of cross-cultural issues. The opinions expressed with regard to these preferences, however, and any mistakes of fact are entirely ours.

We acknowledge the contribution of the members of Canning's cross-cultural team – in particular Richard Pooley, Nigel White and Gerard Bannon – and of the many unnamed clients whose real-life experiences form the basis of this book. We would also like to express our gratitude to all our other colleagues and friends who have inspired, encouraged and helped us: Sharon Davies for patiently checking the manuscript before it was sent to the publishers; Richard Griffiths, John King, Jill Madden, Krystina Mecner, Andrew Shaw, James Shirreff, Kim Taylor, Gary Walker and Roz Wynter-Bee for sharing their international business experiences with us; Elizabeth Bawdon and Michael Norris for their perceptive comments on international presentations; the late and much-missed Ivan Hill for his insights into Scandinavian culture; and Dr Jehad al Omari for allowing us to include his comments about the Arab world. We also thank Sandy Macdonald and Murray Robertson for reading and commenting on the text.

Introduction

Every year at Canning we meet around 5,000 managers from all over the globe. They come from large corporations, middle-sized niche companies and small consultancy firms in a wide range of sectors. Some of them are in the early stages of their career; others have already climbed to the top of the ladder. Some of them work behind the scenes – for example, in an R&D lab or the back-office of a bank; others are out in the field trying to find new customers, or seeking out prospective joint venture partners; and an increasing number are being sent abroad to lead turn-key projects or manage a foreign team. No matter where they work or what they do, they all have one thing in common: as the globalization process gathers momentum, their contact with people from other countries is becoming ever more frequent; and they have found that the more national borders their companies cross, the greater the scope for misunderstanding and conflict.

Every day we hear stories about arrogant foreign bosses who make unreasonable demands; counterparts who seem to take real pleasure in being obstructive or devious; audiences who unexpectedly react to a presenter's proposals with hostility and aggression; negotiating partners who try to deceive or, for no apparent reason, cancel a deal at the last moment. And as our clients describe these situations to us, their frustration – and often, anguish – is plain to see. Sometimes, of course, their international partners are indeed being arrogant, devious or deliberately obstructive. Most of the time, however, communications break down because there's a culture gap that neither side is aware of; or because compatriots back home at head office won't allow their managers in the field to adapt corporate policy to suit local needs.

This book is based on the real business situations our international clients have described to us. Below is a typical example:

A Swedish company had established very clear global purchasing guidelines: no more than 30 per cent of any particular item could be supplied by one vendor; quotes had to be obtained from at least three different suppliers, and contracts were to be awarded purely on the basis of price, delivery terms, reliability and quality. Anders, the Swedish regional manager for South-East Asia, was disturbed to note that, despite several reminders, the subsidiary in Vietnam did not appear to be following these guidelines. In fact, the range of suppliers they used seemed to be very limited, and most of them were Chinese. The subsidiary's Chinese manager seemed very unconcerned when Anders raised this problem with him. 'Well, of course most of our suppliers are Chinese', he said. 'I only use vendors I'm related to.' When Anders explained that this practice would have to stop because it was unethical and anti-competitive, the Chinese manager was genuinely puzzled: 'But I can't see what the problem is', he said. 'My family are much more loyal and reliable than people I don't know. I can call them any time of day or night. They can't escape me. And, of course, they give me much better discounts. Surely you don't want me to use suppliers I don't trust.'

Who do you identify with here? Anders who was convinced that nepotism was unequivocally wrong, or the Chinese manager who regarded giving contracts to his family as a perfectly normal, logical and acceptable thing to do? If you were Anders, what would you do next? And what impact do you think your instinctive response would be likely to have on the Chinese manager? There are clearly a number of cultural differences that could affect the outcome of this situation. But what are they? And what lies behind them? These are the kinds of questions we ask you as each short business scenario unfolds. And to help you answer them, we invite you to place yourself – and your foreign business partners – on a series of cultural preference scales. For example:

Fixed truth						Relative truth				
There are clear rights and wrongs.						What is right and wrong depends on the circumstances.				
50	40	30	20	10	0	10	20	30	40	50

We then offer you practical advice on how best you can bridge the gap when the person you're dealing with falls at the opposite end of the scale from you. The scales are designed to help you gradually build up a picture of how your own culture differs from others and why. For that reason, we suggest that you read the chapters in the order that they appear – at least, for the first time. If you start with, say, Chapter 3 – which is where you'll find out how Anders responded to his Chinese subordinate's purchasing policy – you will have missed some key steps in the argument.

Each of the cultural preference scales is necessarily two-dimensional. And when, for example, we tell you that, in our experience, the Americans lean to the left of a scale and members of the Arab world to the right, we realize that this is a sweeping generalization. There is huge cultural diversity among the United States' 300 million inhabitants; and there are considerable differences between, say, the Saudis and the Egyptians. In making these generalizations, our aim is simply to start you thinking about the broad impact a particular society's history, politics, social structures, education and so on are likely to have on its members' beliefs, attitudes and behaviour.

The first four chapters focus on bridging the culture gap during day-to-day communications – both inside and outside the global organization – with managers, colleagues, subordinates, suppliers and clients. Chapters 5 and 6 look at ways in which you can adapt your presentation and negotiation skills to suit the expectations of your international audiences and partners. Chapter 7 shows you how to speak Offshore English – in other words, how to make yourself understood when you are using the international business community's lingua franca. And in Chapter 8, the cultural preference scales – plus lists of DOs and DON'Ts that summarize and expand on the practical advice from the previous chapters – are brought together under five key headings: relationships, communication, time, truth, and the meaning of life.

The business situations you will find in every chapter are real; but, with one or two exceptions, the names of the companies and managers in them are invented. For the most part, we have used first names – even for people from cultures where addressing colleagues more formally is the norm. That's because *Takashi's project*, *Pascale's client*, or *Helmut's presentation* is much easier to read and remember than *Watanabe-san's project*, *Madame Carpentier's client* or *Herr Doktor Baldauf's presentation*. Where we felt a company's identity could be too easily guessed, we have disguised or changed its size and sector. Occasionally, we give you a short script of how a conversation went; while these scripts are faithful to the spirit of what was said, they are not verbatim.

No writer on cross-cultural matters can be objective. Your writers are both British. Penny is English, and Chris is Welsh. Between us, we have over 40 years' experience of working with people from other countries. Even so, we recognize that every opinion we offer reflects our own cultural conditioning. We have tried very hard to make sure that these opinions are not expressions of prejudice, and apologize in advance to any individual who feels offended. It's worth remembering that you, the reader, can't be objective either. The way you interpret what we have written will be strongly influenced by your own cultural conditioning.

We are aware that you may come from one of over 200 nationalities and that English may not be your native tongue. We have tried to keep our language as straightforward as possible, without making it too simplistic for our native-speaking readers. Occasionally, we have felt the need to use a word or phrase that, in our experience, a high intermediate non-native speaker would be unlikely to recognize or guess from the context. In such cases, we offer a simpler – but less colourful – 'Offshore English' alternative in brackets next to the word. If you're a native speaker, please *bear with us* (be patient). When you reach Chapter 7, you will discover why your international partners would find it hard to understand you if you used such an expression yourself; and why using language sensitively is one of the key skills for anyone who wishes to bridge the culture gap.

1 Interpreting the party line

By uniting we stand, by dividing we fall.
(John Dickinson, *The Liberty Song*, 1768)

Customers, shareholders and the media soon lose faith and interest in a company that projects a confused or inconsistent image. Which is why every business strives to present itself to the outside world as a united entity with a single set of beliefs. The trouble is, the bigger a company becomes and the more national borders it crosses, the harder it has to work to preserve the united front that is so vital to its continued prosperity.

For many multinationals, developing everything centrally – such as the messages they want to broadcast and the brands they market – is the only answer. This central norm or *party line* is then disseminated throughout the organization. This can work if the people at HQ are prepared to adapt the party line to suit local needs – and if their colleagues in the foreign subsidiaries are willing to keep an open mind. All too often, however, everyone assumes that their own attitudes and beliefs are universal, right and normal. *It doesn't even occur to them* (the idea doesn't enter their heads) that people from other cultures might see things from a different perspective.

It's only natural to regard your own view of the world as the right one; and to believe that anyone who doesn't share it is strange or unusual. But there's no such thing as normal. Which is why party lines can cause so much misunderstanding, conflict and stress – both for the people who are trying to disseminate them, and for those on the receiving end. The people at head office jump to the conclusion that the subsidiaries are being deliberately difficult or obstructive; and the people in the subsidiaries automatically assume that their foreign bosses are arrogant megalomaniacs who simply don't care about the problems their directives are causing.

Clearly, there will be times when your international colleagues are indeed being arrogant or deliberately obstructive. Often, however, they will simply be trying to do what they genuinely believe is best for all concerned. It's easy to jump to negative conclusions about other people's motives if you measure what they do and say against your own cultural norms. But not everyone looks at mission statements and corporate initiatives in the same way as you do; another culture's working rhythm may be very different from yours; and your natural communication style could well seem brusque – or excessively indirect – to some of your foreign colleagues.

Mission statements

At its most general and abstract, the party line is often declared publicly in the company's mission statement. As you might expect, however, not everyone interprets it in the spirit that head office intends:

When three large engineering firms – two from Northern Europe and one from the United States – merged, they invested a lot of time, money and resources in producing the new company's mission statement. At a seminar designed to bring middle management together, the top directors invited delegates to explain how they had disseminated the new core values among their local employees.

Each of the Northern European countries involved (Germany, Finland, Sweden) had presented the statement to their teams at a series of short meetings held during working hours. The teams had discussed the core values briefly, and that was that. To their embarrassment, very few of the managers on the seminar could remember them in any detail.

The Americans, on the other hand, had met regularly, outside working hours, to discuss what the new core values meant to each of them. They had translated the abstract aims into concrete guidelines which they could relate to their daily work. Everyone carried a copy of the statement with them at all times and consulted it regularly.

Each side had been very surprised to hear the other's approach. After a few beers in the bar at the end of the day, one of the Finns leaned across to one of the Americans and said: 'What you said about the mission statement – that was just bullshit for the board, wasn't it?' The American was astonished. 'No', he replied. 'Why would you think that?'

It was unthinkable to the Northern Europeans that the Americans could take the mission statement so seriously. Equally, it was unthinkable to the Americans that the Northern Europeans could dismiss it so casually. Of course, the two firms had only recently merged; so these two groups of managers *were bound to be* (couldn't avoid being) influenced by their pre-merger ways of doing things. But that doesn't explain why there was such a wide gap in their perceptions on this particular issue. It's highly likely that cultural conditioning was also playing a major part here.

Have a look at the pair of statements below:

Theoretical						Empirical				
I like using abstract concepts to solve problems.						For me, concrete experience is more important than theory.				
50	40	30	20	10	0	10	20	30	40	50

Think about them in relation to your working life, and what you personally value and try to achieve. Then decide where you would place yourself on the scales: on 50 at one end or the other? Or somewhere in between?

Mission statements often say things like:

We believe that the Zoetica brand must represent a positive force in the world. We will act in line with this belief at all times.

or

We believe in the integrity of human beings, and will treat our employees, customers and anyone coming into contact with Zoetica accordingly, inviting them all to be part of the Zoetica family.

These are, of course, honourable sentiments that no reasonable person could object to. The trouble is, they're framed in very abstract terms. But then, of course, they have to be. A company can't make a concrete and meaningful statement of intent and values without losing flexibility. And flexibility is what businesses need if they are to survive. They've got to be able to take decisions quickly, and act upon them right away. They've got to retain absolute flexibility to diversify, downsize, grow, and so on.

The American managers in this situation would probably lean towards the theoretical end of the scale. They took the abstract values expressed in the mission statement very seriously and were prepared to spend their own time discussing them in depth. They had no trouble translating these general theories into concrete, practical guidelines that they could relate to their daily work. If you like using abstract concepts to solve problems, you may well respond to your company's mission statement as positively as these American managers did.

If, on the other hand, you lean towards the empirical end of the scale, you may find it hard to take this kind of abstract theorizing seriously. The Northern European managers here discussed the core values briefly and dismissed them as meaningless. What possible relevance could they have to their daily working lives? We recently asked the German HR manager of a large multinational how she felt about her company's mission statement. She said: 'Well, we have to have one. It's good PR. But, in practical terms, it isn't worth the paper it's written on.' The Northern Europeans would probably share her view. That's why they couldn't even remember in any detail what the mission statement said; and why the Finnish manager was convinced that the American managers' explanation of how they had disseminated the new core values was *just bullshit for the board*.

We're not trying to suggest that all Americans would lean to the left of this scale; nor that all Northern Europeans would fall to the right. But there's no denying that attitudes towards mission statements do vary considerably from culture to culture. And when an empiricist meets a theorist there's considerable scope for misunderstanding.

Corporate initiatives

There's no way you can undo a lifetime's conditioning, of course. But, when you're working internationally, you have to make some effort to understand and adapt to the way different cultures see things. If not, the company's attempts to project a consistent and harmonious external image will lead to considerable conflict and disharmony internally:

The American HQ of an international chemicals company produced a 'quality chart' which included the following statement: 'Each and every one of us will take responsibility for the quality of our products.' They sent the chart to the Belgian, French, German and UK subsidiaries, and asked them to sign it and send it back.

The Belgians, the British and the Germans complied with the request straight away. But nothing was received from the French. Several e-mails were sent to chase it up, but these remained unanswered. Finally Harvey (the American boss) called Luc (the French manager) to find out what was going on. The conversation went something like this:

Harvey: I'm calling about the quality initiative. Did you get the chart we sent you last month?

Luc: Yes.

Harvey: Oh you did get it. Good. So could you get everyone to sign it and send it back to us? By the end of the week, if you can.

Luc: Well, no, I'm afraid I can't. I've discussed it with the team and none of us is willing to sign it.

Harvey: Not willing? Why not?

Luc: We don't agree with it.

Harvey: You don't agree with it?

Luc: No.

Harvey: But it isn't a question of agreement. All we're asking for is your buy-in.

Luc: Yes and, as I said, we can't do that. It's not logical. Production and quality control are in Belgium.

Harvey: What difference does that make?

Luc: How can we be held responsible for something we have no control over?

Harvey: No one's going to hold you responsible. We're just asking you to pledge yourselves to the global quality initiative.

Luc: But the document clearly says: 'Each and every one of us will take responsibility for the quality of our products.' We can't possibly sign it.

Harvey and Luc discussed this question again several times, without success. Luc and his colleagues refused to be moved and their relations with the Americans grew increasingly hostile. *Eventually* (finally), the Belgian country manager intervened and suggested a compromise that both sides were prepared to accept. Luc and his colleagues would sign the quality chart if Harvey gave them a written assurance that they wouldn't be held contractually responsible for the aims that were stated in it. Harvey thought this was obvious and couldn't understand why they were being so difficult. The French were equally perplexed: 'In that case,' they said, 'the chart is meaningless. So why are you issuing it?' Relations between the two countries remained hostile for some time.

There's no doubt in our minds that Luc and his team were as committed to product quality as Harvey was. So why did this corporate initiative lead to so much misunderstanding and resentment? At first sight, the whole situation is very puzzling. The United States is famous for having an extremely litigious culture: few business deals are finalized until the lawyers have drawn up a detailed contract that covers every possible eventuality; people will usually only sign a contract if they're confident it is *watertight* (comprehensive and impossible to misinterpret); they will tend to consult it regularly throughout the life of the deal; and partners who fail to honour their contractual obligations will most probably be threatened with legal action. So why didn't Harvey understand Luc's reluctance to sign the quality chart?

Well, most of the international business people we work with would agree that the United States also has a forward-looking culture where taking an optimistic, upbeat approach is the norm; and where people feel fairly comfortable stating their beliefs, hopes and intentions both openly and publicly. When Harvey was at school, for example, he and his classmates started each day by putting their hands on their hearts and pledging their allegiance to the flag of the United States of America. For him, publicly confirming your commitment to quality is similar to pledging yourself to 'one Nation under God, indivisible, with liberty and justice for all'. So it simply didn't occur to him that anyone would regard the chart as a legal contract. That's why he was so puzzled when Luc said he didn't agree with it: 'But it isn't a question of agreement. All we're asking for is your buy-in'; and 'We're just asking you to pledge yourselves to the global quality initiative.' But, of course, Luc isn't a native English speaker and the subtle vocabulary differences meant nothing to him. As far as he was concerned, Harvey was asking him to agree to take responsibility for something he had no control over.

Luc tried very hard to explain his position, but Harvey didn't seem to register what he was saying. That may be because the two colleagues would lean towards opposite ends of this scale:

Analytical	Intuitive
What I value most is a logical, comprehensive and consistent argument. Even if I instinctively feel a proposal is right, I need to test every step in the argument before I can commit myself.	What I value most are creative and intriguing ideas that appeal to the emotions. If I instinctively feel a proposal is right, I don't need to test every single step in the argument before I commit myself.

50	40	30	20	10	0	10	20	30	40	50

As soon as they received the quality chart, the analytical French immediately tested the logic of what they were being asked to do. The wording was clear and unambiguous: 'Each and every one of us will take responsibility for the quality of our products.' Clearly, then, if they signed the chart, it would have the force of a contract. If there were a quality failure, they would be in breach of that contract. And Luc and his team could end up losing their jobs as a result. But quality control was in Belgium. So there was no way they could be held responsible. Straight Cartesian logic. And because Harvey refused to acknowledge their argument, the French immediately suspected his motives. This was obviously a devious head office plot to cut headcount without making redundancy payments.

Harvey's approach to the quality chart was far more intuitive. Committing yourself to product quality was unquestionably the right thing to do. Sure, production and quality control were in Belgium. So obviously the French couldn't be held responsible for problems that arose there. But that didn't prevent them from monitoring customer satisfaction and responding fast and efficiently to complaints. And that was all he was expecting them to do.

So what could Harvey have done to avoid all this unnecessary drama and ill-will? Well, have another look at the way he handled the phone call to Luc. He didn't make much effort to find out what Luc's concerns really were, did he? He was far too busy concentrating on himself and what he wanted. As a result, he pushed all the wrong buttons.

According to American anthropologist, Edward T Hall (*Understanding Cultural Differences*, 1989):

> The essence of effective cross-cultural communication is more to do with releasing the right responses than with sending the right messages.

In other words, you've got to push the *right* buttons. To do that, you need to keep an open mind, try to put yourself in the other person's position, ask perceptive questions, and really listen to *what* they are saying and *how* they sound when they say it.

If Harvey had done that, the conversation might have gone very differently:

Harvey: I'm calling about the quality chart. ¹*Did you have a chance to discuss it with your people yet?*

Luc: Oh yes. We've discussed it in great detail.

Harvey: OK... ²*And how do they feel about it?*

Luc: It's caused quite a few problems here, to be honest.

Harvey: Really? ³*What kind of problems?*

Luc: Well, we don't see how you can hold us responsible for something we have no control over.

Harvey: But... ⁴*You know, Luc, I think there's some kind of misunderstanding here. Tell me, what is it you feel you have no control over?*

Luc: It's not a feeling. It's a fact. The Belgians are responsible for product quality, not us. So we can't sign a contract that says: 'Each and every one of us will take responsibility for the quality of our products.' It isn't logical.

Harvey: ⁵*You mean your people see this chart as a contract?*

Luc: Yes, of course. Isn't that what it is?

Harvey: Well, no. There's nothing legally binding about it. It's just an acknowledgement of what I hope we all believe in anyway.

Luc: So why do you want us to sign it?

Harvey: Well, it's what we normally do here in the States. It's a kind of symbolic gesture. You know, a way of pledging support for the company's aims... ⁶*But I guess you guys thought there was some kind of sinister motive behind it. Right?*

Luc: Well, yes. People are very worried about losing their jobs, through no fault of their own.

Harvey: Losing their jobs? Well, Luc, let me assure you that simply isn't going to happen... Listen, how about if I come over and...

In the first conversation, Harvey concentrated on his own agenda. This time he focuses on Luc and his team. [1]*Did you have a chance to discuss it with your people yet?* elicits a much more useful response than *Could you get everyone to sign it and send it back to us?* From what Luc says, and probably his tone of voice too, Harvey realizes that something is wrong.

So he follows up with a couple of **open questions** (ones that start with *who, what, why, where, how,* etc) to try to find out more: [2]*And how do they feel about it?*; [3]*What kind of problems?*

Luc's reply surprises him and, at first, he instinctively wants to contradict him – *But no one's going to hold you responsible* – as he did in the first conversation. Fortunately, he stops himself just in time, acknowledges that there may be a problem of interpretation here, and probes further with another **open question**: [4]*You know, Luc, I think there's some kind of misunderstanding here. Tell me, what is it you feel you have no control over?*

In his reply, Luc refers to the quality chart as a *contract*. This is just what Harvey needs to know. But he's very surprised. So he asks a closed question (one that invites a *Yes* or *No* answer) to check that he has understood Luc correctly: [5]*You mean your people see this chart as a contract?*

Because Harvey shows interest and a willingness to understand, Luc is beginning to feel less defensive and now asks a **closed question** himself: *Isn't that what it is?* Negative questions – *Don't you like it? Can't you do it? Didn't it work?* – are often used to show surprise. So what Luc means is: *I'm very surprised to hear you say it isn't a contract, because that's certainly what we all think it is.*

When Harvey reassures Luc that there's nothing legally binding about the chart, Luc asks: *So why do you want us to sign it?* Harvey could get angry or exasperated here. But he doesn't. He tries to work out where Luc is coming from. This is a key moment in the conversation. It's when the fog really starts to clear for Harvey. He explains what the chart means to him as clearly as he can. And then asks a **closed question** to check that he has correctly deduced how the French feel about it: [6]*But I guess you guys thought there was some kind of sinister motive behind it. Right?*

Once Harvey knows that Luc and his colleagues are worried about losing their jobs, he realizes how much damage this seemingly uncontroversial corporate initiative has done to morale in the French subsidiary. And he can start trying to put things right.

Implementing corporate initiatives is never easy. And there's no magic formula that will guarantee success. But because Harvey was prepared to question his own assumptions and make an effort to put himself in Luc's position, the two colleagues now understand one another much better than they did before. And there's a good chance that harmonious relations between head office and subsidiary will be re-established.

Working rhythms

The need to present a united front makes life difficult for everyone: the people like Harvey who are trying to disseminate a party line; and the people like Luc who are on the receiving end. If you work in a subsidiary, you may end up regarding the people from HQ as *corporate seagulls*: they fly in, shit on you from on high, and fly out again. It's hard enough to resist HQ diktats when they are imposed from afar. It's even harder when the corporate seagull builds a nest in your workplace. This is exactly what happened at the Irish production facility of a Swiss multinational:

When the head of the Irish plant resigned, the Swiss decided to parachute in one of their own people. The new Swiss manager's office was very close to the canteen and he was disturbed to note that the Irish employees were going for frequent and extensive coffee breaks. Instead of taking just one 10-minute break in the morning, and one in the afternoon – which was what happened in Switzerland – they seemed to go to the canteen whenever they felt like it, and to sit around laughing and joking with their friends for 20 minutes at a time.

The new Swiss manager decided that something would have to be done to stop all this time-wasting. So he made a unilateral decision to install coffee-making equipment in every department; and announced that, in future, the canteen would only open at lunchtime.

The Irish employees were not impressed by the new party line. Far from wasting time under the old regime, they had spent their coffee breaks sharing departmental news, asking advice and generally networking. When this forum was closed down, interdepartmental communication started to deteriorate. It wasn't long before productivity at this, the company's biggest plant, started to go down.

The Swiss, of course, are famous for their attachment to time. And this new manager was clearly no exception. In fact, he would probably place himself to the far left of this scale:

Monochronic						Polychronic				
I prefer to deal with one task at a time in a structured fashion.						I prefer to have several tasks running at the same time.				
50	40	30	20	10	0	10	20	30	40	50

If you're from a monochronic culture too, you may find that you instinctively do one thing after another, in a linear fashion. And you probably feel that unless each moment is used for a specific purpose, it's wasted. If, on the other hand, you lean towards the polychronic end of the scale, you may well regard time as more elastic. Dr Jehad al-Omari – a Jordanian author of books on Arab business culture – is one of Canning's associate training consultants. This is what he told us:

> In the Arab world it is timing rather than time that is important. In the West, when you invite people for drinks at 7.30 pm and dinner at 8.00 pm you expect them to arrive at that time. Among Arabs, you serve dinner when the time is right, when everyone is comfortable and ready to eat. You follow the mood rather than the schedule. It's the same thing when you have to break bad news. You don't do it straight away. You wait until the time is right – when the person is ready to take it.

Very different from the Swiss Germans (and, indeed, the Germans), who tend to plan their time in a very structured and ordered way. As they work out *Die Tagesordnung* (the Daily Order), they will often allot a specific and precise amount of time to each task – including their coffee breaks. So while the Irish aren't particularly polychronic – you certainly wouldn't put them in the same category as members of the Arab world – they do lie to the right of the Swiss on this scale. As a result, their working rhythms are more relaxed. That's not to say they get less done than their Swiss counterparts. They just use their time in a different way. And that was probably the underlying cause of this misunderstanding.

But there is a puzzling aspect to this situation. As you will see in Chapter 2, business hierarchies in both Ireland and Switzerland are relatively flat. And in flat business cultures, bosses tend to consult widely, and subordinates generally feel free to express their own views fairly openly. So why didn't that happen here? Why did the new Swiss manager behave in such an autocratic way? And why didn't his Irish subordinates challenge his decision?

Maybe the Swiss guy simply panicked. It's not easy taking over as manager of a foreign subsidiary. When you first arrive in a new country, everything strikes you as very strange. The way people do things seems completely different from the way you do things back home. You can feel so dislocated that you fail to notice the many similarities between where you are and where you come from. What the Swiss manager saw was an undisciplined workforce who seemed to be *blatantly* (very openly) taking advantage of the management's goodwill. While he wouldn't have behaved so autocratically back home, he probably felt it was the only thing he could do under these strange new circumstances.

But what about the Irish? Why didn't someone try to explain how useful the coffee breaks were? Well, perhaps they regarded HQ with suspicion and resentment. People in an overseas subsidiary often do, as you will know if you have ever worked in one. Complaints like: *They have no idea of the conditions over here, and they're not interested*; *all they ever do is issue instructions*; *they never ask us what we think* are commonplace. If this was how the Irish employees felt, they would have seen no point in challenging the new boss's diktat. He was just doing what people from HQ had always done: shitting on them from on high.

The lack of communication in this situation had a damaging effect on all concerned: the Irish, the Swiss boss and the company. If you are being asked to accept a party line that conflicts with the way you do things in your part of the world, don't just assume that HQ's motives are sinister, or that the sole purpose of the directive is to make your life difficult. Try to find out what's behind it. Ask some questions, and listen to the answers with an open mind. However hard it may be, try for a moment to put yourself in HQ's position. And then, as clearly, calmly and objectively as you can, explain your own position and the impact that the new directive will have on you and your colleagues. This won't guarantee success, of course. But it has to be more productive than keeping quiet and letting things go from bad to worse.

Communication styles

It's a problem that confronts the corporate seagull all too often. You arrive at the subsidiary, issue your instructions, and then later discover that everyone has completely ignored them:

A large French company decided to introduce a new global purchasing policy. In the past, subsidiaries had sourced many of their supplies locally. In future, they would be expected, where possible, to use the same suppliers as the French parent company. The French purchasing manager visited the subsidiaries one by one to explain the new arrangements. In each case, she presented the facts and figures very clearly, and made sure the purchasing teams were fully aware of the considerable cost savings that would be achieved.

She had been expecting a certain amount of resistance from the Japanese subsidiary. So she wasn't particularly worried by the surprised glances and exhalations of breath that greeted her announcement. Nor was she unduly concerned when one of the team said: 'This will be very difficult for us.' After all, they were bound to say that. The important thing was that no one rejected the proposals. She went home feeling relatively pleased with herself.

Six months later, she was surprised to see that the Japanese had not made one single purchase through the new system. She phoned Tokyo to find out what was going on. Her colleague said: 'We made it very clear, when you were here, that we couldn't use this new system.'

It's hard to believe that they were all present at the same meeting, isn't it? So what went wrong here? Were the Japanese being deliberately two-faced and underhand? Did they think that if they pretended to go along with the joint purchasing project to the French woman's face, they could simply ignore it once she had gone back to France? And what about the French woman? Was she being arrogant, or just incredibly obtuse? Well, in all probability, both sides were behaving in what they regarded as a professional and straightforward way. The Japanese thought they had made it perfectly clear that they couldn't source their supplies from France. The French woman was equally sure that the Japanese had no serious objections to the new arrangements. It was just that their understanding of the word *difficult* was not the same.

The Japanese impulse is to preserve harmony. For them, consensus rather than open disagreement or conflict is the name of the game, and their communication style reflects this. In this cultural context the word *difficult*, accompanied by eye and body language that every other Japanese would immediately understand, means: *This is absolutely out of the question. There's no way we can agree to this*. But when the French say *difficult* they mean: *Not easy, but not impossible either.*

Have a look at this pair of statements:

Low context	High context
Business relationships are complicated. Therefore, communication needs to be frank, explicit and direct.	Business relationships are complicated. Therefore, communication needs to be diplomatic, implicit and indirect.

50	40	30	20	10	0	10	20	30	40	50

Edward T Hall – the American anthropologist we referred to earlier – divides the cultures of the world into low context and high context communicators and a number of cross-cultural experts have adopted his terminology. Low context communicators tend to express themselves in explicit, concrete, unequivocal terms. There's little cultural baggage or 'context' attached to the words they use and you can usually take what they say at face value. If you are, for example, American, German, Scandinavian or Finnish, you will probably fall into this category. And when you're doing business with other low context communicators, you will probably find their communication style reassuringly straightforward and comprehensible.

High context communicators, on the other hand, tend to communicate more implicitly. They expect you to be able to interpret what they mean from your knowledge of the cultural values that lie behind the words, what they're actually talking about at the time, their tone of voice and, of course, their eye and body language. Interestingly enough, both the French and the Japanese would fall well to the right of this scale. But, of course, their cultural contexts are different. You may be a high con-text communicator yourself, but that won't necessarily make it any easier for you to understand a high context communicator from another culture.

It didn't occur to the French woman to check that she had understood her Japanese colleagues correctly. As a result, a lot of time and money was wasted and HQ's relations with their subsidiary were disrupted. If you're a corporate seagull, you can learn from her mistake. Don't take what the people in your subsidiaries say at face value. Watch their body language too. If she had taken notice of those surprised glances and exhalations of breath, the French woman would have realized that her Japanese colleagues weren't prepared to accept her proposals.

Making sure you understand exactly what the other person means won't guarantee success. But at least you will know where you stand. In this situation, for example, the Japanese refused to accept the party line because they were worried about quality. If this concern had been brought out into the open, the French could have discussed it objectively with their Japanese partners, and tried to find ways to overcome their concerns.

In *Working rhythms* above, we looked at the difficulties a Swiss manager had when he banned coffee breaks in an Irish plant. The Irish clearly have a more relaxed attitude towards time than the Swiss. And this may well have been one of the reasons the problem arose. But the misunderstanding was most probably compounded by their differing communication styles.

The Swiss are low context communicators. In fact, they generally fall to the far left of this scale, while the Irish (along with the British) would lean towards the right. And when a low context communicator meets a higher context communicator, they may both misinterpret the signals the other is sending. When the Swiss guy gave the Irish the bad news about coffee breaks, he probably did so in very frank and explicit terms:

You are wasting too much time laughing and joking in the canteen when you should be working at your desks. This is completely unacceptable. In future, the canteen will only open at lunchtime. You will find coffee-making equipment in your department. Please remember that you are allowed one 10-minute break in the morning and one in the afternoon.

But this approach would have come across to the Irish as autocratic, impersonal and cold. When we described this situation to Padraig, an Irish business acquaintance of ours from Dublin, he told us that if the Irish have bad news to give, they generally try to *sugar the pill* (sweeten the medicine). He illustrated his point by telling us the following joke:

A tourist approaches two fellows and ask them how far it is to the town. The first fellow assures the tourist it's just two miles down the road. The tourist thanks them and goes off. The second fellow then says: 'Why did you tell him that? Don't you know that it's four miles?' To which his friend replies: 'Sure I know, but the poor man is walking.'

As you will see from the other chapters in this book, differing communication styles are a major cause of misunderstanding in the international arena.

Summary

There are those who will tell you that a process called 'globalization' is creating an environment in which companies can operate virtually anywhere in the world under identical conditions to those back home. This is a dangerous belief. It leads people to assume that there is one norm, one way of doing things, one way of looking at the world. As the people in the situations we have looked at discovered, there is no such thing as normal.

When you are doing business with different cultures, there will almost certainly be a gap, of one kind or another, between your perceptions and theirs. This need not stop you presenting a united front. The key to success is to acknowledge that there is a gap and to make genuine attempts to bridge it. The most successful cross-cultural communicators are those who are instinctively able to push the right buttons. To follow their example, you need to:

■ keep an open mind;

■ try to put yourself in the other person's position;

■ ask carefully chosen **open questions** (ones that start with who, what, why, where, how, etc);

■ really listen to the answers;

■ ask **closed** questions (ones that invite a Yes or No answer) to check that any deductions you've made are correct.

2 Knowing your place

All men, if they work not as in the great taskmaster's eye, will work wrong, and work unhappily for themselves and for you.

(Thomas Carlyle, *Past and Present*, 1843)

The multinational organization may need to present a united front to the outside world, but in your daily business life you will be dealing with people who work behind that front. A dynamic company is similar to a healthy political system. If it is to move forward and grow, it needs internal diversity and competition. But, of course, these diverse individuals and competing groups have to be kept on track; synergies have to be achieved; consensus has to be reached; and final decisions have to be taken. Which is why virtually every organization – no matter how small – has some kind of chain of command.

Most companies make an attempt to show how the hierarchy works by producing an organization chart. This will certainly show you who is nominally responsible for what, and who reports to who. But how accurately does it reflect what happens on a day-to-day basis? Does it tell you, for example, what the balance of power really is, how far an individual's authority or responsibilities extend, how much autonomy the people involved enjoy? Can you see, at a glance, how decisions are made, where an individual's loyalties lie, who you should talk to when you want to get things done and, most importantly, how your colleagues expect to be treated? In our experience, it does not.

Imagine, for a moment, that you work in a company where there are five levels of management. You are at level 4 in department A. Your department works fairly closely with department B:

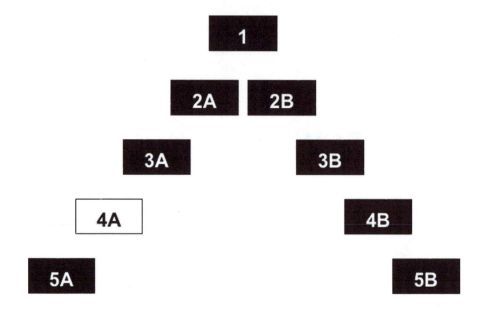

So 5A reports to you. You report to 3A. And so on. 5A needs 5B to do some urgent work for her by the end of the week. 5B has told her he hasn't got time. What would you expect your reportee to do? Should she:

- speak to 5B again and persuade him that the work has to be done?
- ask you to speak to 5B?
- ask you to speak to 4B?
- speak directly to 4B herself?

And what if you urgently need authorization to make a substantial change to the budget and your boss (3A) is away. How comfortable would you feel about talking directly to 2A, or even 1, about it?

Of course, a lot will depend on how big your company is and on how well you get on with the various personalities involved. But the way you instinctively answer these questions will also be influenced by where you come from. When you're on home territory, you will usually know your place, and are aware of how your colleagues expect you to behave. But once you step outside your own corporate and national culture, you may well find people whose expectations and behaviour are very different from yours. Once again, there's no such thing as normal. Attitudes towards handling the hierarchy, taking responsibility, monitoring performance and getting colleagues to *play ball* (cooperate) will vary from culture to culture.

Handling the hierarchy

How you handle the hierarchy will, to some extent, depend on where you would place yourself on the following scale:

Flat hierarchy						Vertical hierarchy				
Leaders should share power.						Leaders should hold power.				
50	40	30	20	10	0	10	20	30	40	50

If you expect your leaders to hold rather than share their power, you may well believe that when 5A wants to get 5B to do some urgent work for her, she should refer to her boss (4A). He can then ask 4B to tell his reportee (5B) what to do. If, on the other hand, you believe your leaders should share power, you would probably expect 5A to speak directly to 5B without getting the bosses involved.

When you're working with people whose culture seems to have little in common with yours, there's always a temptation to believe that they will do *everything* differently. But, as some of our clients have discovered, that's not always the case:

Since 2000, Canning has been working with the Renault–Nissan Alliance – first in France and later in Tokyo – to promote greater cultural understanding between French and Japanese colleagues. In the early days of the Alliance, a group of French engineers in Paris told our colleague, Richard Pooley, that it wasn't always easy to get their counterparts in Tokyo to play ball. The Japanese would listen carefully to what the French said and assure them that action would be taken; but then weeks would go by and nothing would happen. A little later, during a cross-cultural seminar in Tokyo, a group of Japanese engineers made very similar comments about their French counterparts. In both cases, our colleagues responded by sketching this diagram on the flipchart:

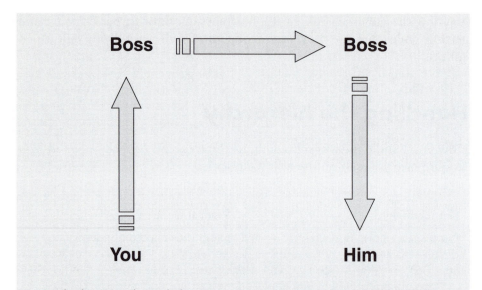

Both the French and the Japanese engineers immediately understood what they meant. 'Ask your boss to speak to 5B's boss.' In other words, handle the hierarchy in just the same way as you do at home. Both groups were equally astonished: 'Why on earth didn't we think of that?'

Well because, in many respects, the culture gap between the French and the Japanese is fairly wide. So it didn't occur to them that, on this particular issue, their approach would be so similar. But the French and the Japanese – along with people from Spain, Latin America, South-East Asia, India and Africa – would lean towards the right of the hierarchy scale. And if you want to get a counterpart to play ball, you will probably need to get the bosses involved.

If this French automotive giant had entered into a joint venture with some fellow Europeans – Brits, Scandinavians or Dutch, for example – they probably wouldn't have expected their new partners' approach to the hierarchy to be any *different* from theirs. But, in fact, business hierarchies in the United Kingdom, Northern Europe and the United States tend to be fairly flat; people are used to being able to challenge their leaders' decisions; they expect their boss to consult them, not issue diktats from on high; and if their colleagues are being troublesome, they tend to tackle them directly. If one of our colleagues in Canning UK played the hierarchy in the French or Japanese way, your two British writers would probably be pretty upset. That's because, in flatter business cultures, running to the boss every time there's a problem is often seen as *bad form* (socially unacceptable). And colleagues who make a habit of it are likely to become very unpopular.

Of course, France and Japan are not the most vertical cultures you will come across. There are some countries – like India, for example – whose social conditioning places them at the very far right of the hierarchical scale. A British business acquaintance of ours has vivid memories of the first time he went to India on business; he was running his own company in the United Kingdom at the time:

> I was in the middle of a meeting with a customer in Bombay (now called Mumbai) when my fountain pen fell off the table and on to the floor. As I bent down to pick it up my customer shouted 'Peon!' at the top of his voice. I was so startled, I left my pen where it was. A few seconds later, a small barefoot man rushed in and my customer started to reprimand him: 'My guest's pen has fallen to the floor. Why were you not here to pick it up? This is inexcusable. This must not happen again.' Much to my embarrassment, the poor man apologized profusely to me, picked the pen up, and placed it carefully on the table. When I tried to thank him, my customer said: 'There's no need to thank him. That is his job.' I felt very uncomfortable indeed. In the United Kingdom, a boss who spoke to his subordinates in this way would probably be taken to an industrial tribunal.

That's not to say the United Kingdom has the flattest business hierarchies you will find. Richard Pooley, Canning's Managing Director, has equally vivid memories of the first time he went to Sweden in the early 1980s to run a presentation skills course:

> When the participants had finished preparing their first short presentation, I said: 'Now I'd like each of you in turn to stand up in front of the group and deliver your speech. Sven, why don't you go first.' Sven smiled, turned to the rest of the group and said something to them in Swedish. I didn't understand a word of the short discussion that followed. But I noticed that everyone contributed to it. Sven then turned to me, smiled again and said: 'Actually, Richard, if you don't mind, we think Erik should go first.' At the coffee break, I asked the group why they had been so surprised when I asked Sven to go first. They explained that, in Sweden, teachers were always careful not to do anything that would make them appear authoritarian. They realized that who should make the first presentation was a relatively minor issue, and reassured me that my innocent suggestion had not in any way offended them. 'But, you see,' said Sven, 'I couldn't possibly go first without consulting the others. I would have felt that I was pushing myself forward. And that kind of behaviour is totally unacceptable in Sweden.'

Swedish business hierarchies tend to be very flat indeed. In fact you could probably spend several days in a Swedish office without even realizing who the boss was. That's because, as Sven explained to Richard, they are taught from an early age that no one should believe they are better, or worth more, than anyone else. Along with the Danes and Norwegians, the Swedes tend to feel instinctively suspicious of people who push themselves forward, behave extravagantly, or boast about their achievements. Modesty is the personal quality that these three cultures seem to value above all else; and if you describe one of them as 'ordinary', they will probably regard it as a compliment.

Some say that this attitude has its roots in the social code that evolved among Scandinavia's small rural communities. The peasant farmers soon discovered that, if they were to survive the harsh conditions of the late Middle Ages, they needed to work closely together as a group. Such interdependence required considerable equality of effort and reward: a farmer who thought he was better than his neighbours might believe he deserved more than them in return for less effort. Such behaviour would destabilize the community and clearly could not be tolerated. The Lutheran reformation, which was embraced by the Nordic countries in the course of the 16th century, must also have played a significant part in reinforcing the Scandinavians' dislike of immodesty, extravagance and self-glorification.

Whatever its origins, this centuries-old, unwritten social code still exerts a strong influence throughout Scandinavia. In 1933, Danish author Aksel Sandemose published a novel ('A Fugitive Crosses His Tracks') condemning the negative impact these values could have. Unable to accept the petty jealousies and narrow-minded behaviour he perceived in his own home town, he moved to Norway. Jante – the imaginary small Danish port featured in the novel – is based on the home town Sandemose left. Jante's small-minded, envious inhabitants live by their own 'Ten Commandments' – or 'Jante Law' – which include: 'You shall not think you are special; You shall not think you are cleverer than us;' and 'You shall not think you can teach us anything.' Few young Scandinavians today actually read this novel; but most will refer to the 'Jante Law' to explain their culture. As Richard discovered during the presentations seminar in Sweden, people still think it's wrong for individuals to push themselves forward; and many ex-pat Swedes will claim that it was the 'Jante Law' mentality that drove them out of the country.

Australia is another country that celebrates its horizontal power relationships. The Australians have their own version of the 'Jante Law'. They call it 'Tall Poppy Syndrome': because it's the tallest poppy in a field that will be picked first, it's the tallest poppy that is the most vulnerable. In other words, if you behave in an immodest or egotistical way, you will be punished. The Australians have little respect for people who think too highly of themselves. And, in 1999, they showed quite clearly that this feeling runs very deep:

John Howard, who was Prime Minister at that time, wrote a new introduction to the constitution. In it he included the following statement:

'We value excellence.'

It's a line that many countries include in the preamble to their constitution, and that most companies expect to see in their mission statement. But it provoked enormous controversy among the Australians. The media immediately attacked Howard for trying to undermine the 'Tall Poppy Syndrome'. And when, during a radio interview, he said: 'If there's one thing we need to get rid of in this country, it's our Tall Poppy Syndrome', the nation was outraged. In a subsequent referendum, the vast majority voted against the new preamble to the constitution.

To the Australians, striving for individual excellence implied pushing yourself forward or trying to be better than others. And in a society where everyone is equal, such behaviour can be perceived as very divisive. So if you're managing a team of Scandinavians or Australians, remember the 'Jante Law' and 'Tall Poppy Syndrome'. Don't play the *heavy-handed* (autocratic) boss; consult them frequently; and don't be surprised or offended if they challenge your decisions.

Many Indians, on the other hand, have a strong sense of their place in the order of things. The Hindu caste system has resulted in a rigid social stratification which still exists, despite Mahatma Ghandi's best attempts to break it down. And, as the *Bhagavad Gita* dictates, they believe that it's better to do the job you are born to do than the job another was born to do – even if you might do it better. The vertical hierarchy is naturally determined and should not be interfered with or ignored. In the mid-1990s, Canning ran a series of courses for the Steel Authority of India. We worked with a number of different groups of Indian managers. But in each case our brief was the same: to help the participants create and deliver more dynamic and effective in-house training programmes. During the early part of each course, their Canning trainer asked each group a vital question: 'What, in your view, is a manager's job?' All the managers in every group – men and women alike – gave exactly the same unequivocal reply: 'A manager's job is to tell people what to do.' And they were genuinely surprised, and even a little puzzled, when our colleagues suggested that there might be other ways of defining the role. So if you're managing an Indian team, don't expect them to challenge your decisions, or come to you with suggestions of how you might do things better. As far as they're concerned, you're the boss and making decisions is your job.

But where on the hierarchy scale would you expect to find your Polish counterparts: to the left with the Northern Europeans, or to the right like the Japanese or Indians? The way their Polish colleagues handled the hierarchy came as a surprise to some Dutch managers. Sytze, a client of ours, had recently been transferred from head office in Amsterdam to his company's Polish subsidiary:

> I was in Warsaw on a four-month secondment to help set up a new database system. My boss was a Dutch guy called Wim who had been in Poland for a year. During that time, the company had moved from their old office on a factory site in the suburbs to a new, ultra-modern building in the centre of Warsaw. On the original plans for the managers' offices, the doors were solid wood and the wall partitions were opaque. But, at Wim's request, glass doors and panels had been used instead. I soon discovered that my new Polish colleagues hated these 'akwariums'. But no one had said anything to Wim. It was clear that they hoped *I* would tell him. So I did. Wim was amazed. He couldn't understand why they hadn't spoken directly to him; nor could he see why they disliked the glass panels. What was their problem? Did they have something to hide? Later a Polish friend explained that many Poles, even the young ones, are very hierarchical and have learnt not to question authority. Bosses are expected to be rather remote. And discussions with them should be conducted in private, not in an 'akwarium'.

Sytze passed the information on to Wim, went back to his project – and then nearly missed his deadline because he made a few wrong assumptions himself:

> One of my main tasks was to train a young software engineer called Piotr. He was a recent graduate from the prestigious Jagellonian University of Krakow, and extremely bright. I asked him to find out what each department wanted from the new database. I couldn't do it myself as I didn't speak Polish. To show Piotr the kind of information we needed, I gave him a short list of questions as a guide.

Naturally, I assumed he would use his initiative and ask plenty of other questions to check and clarify each department's different needs. But he didn't. In every case, he asked exactly the same questions from the list I had given him. The answers he received were predictable and not nearly detailed enough. We were under a lot of time pressure. Something had to be done, quickly. So, again, I asked my Polish friend for advice: 'Well,' he said, 'as I mentioned before, a lot of Poles are very hierarchical. And, of course, many of the older generation hate being questioned. It probably reminds them of the communist era. You need tell them exactly what Piotr is doing and why he needs to ask them questions. I suggest you write a note in English and send it to all the department heads. As well as explaining what you're doing, it would also be a good idea to emphasize Piotr's qualifications and give the name of his university. A note in English will be treated with respect, and Piotr's academic qualifications will gain him respect too.' I followed his advice and it worked.

The impact of recent history on the way people relate to their bosses and peers should not be underestimated. The Soviet Union may no longer exist, but attitudes that were formed during the communist era continue to influence behaviour at work. Like Sytze and Wim, many Western managers fail to take this into account.

It isn't enough to know whether a culture is flat or vertical. You also need to find out where it falls on the following scale:

Individualist						Group-oriented				
My first duty should be to myself.						My first duty should be to the group I belong to.				
50	40	30	20	10	0	10	20	30	40	50

When Pieter, a South African businessman, secured a major infrastructural contract in Japan, he put together a team of locals from his firm's Japanese subsidiary to run the project. One night he had dinner with the team leader, Yoshinori, a man in his late forties. The conversation was rather flat, so Pieter started talking about the performance of their respective teams in the recent rugby World Cup. 'Your team was absolute rubbish', he said jokingly, and then waited for Yoshinori to make some similar comment about the South Africans. But Yoshinori just nodded and smiled. So Pieter tried again: 'But I guess that's normal. I mean, you don't exactly top the league in any sport, do you?' Again Yoshinori nodded and smiled. Pieter was very frustrated: all red-blooded males enjoy making fun of other people's sporting ability; so why didn't this guy start mocking the South African team? As he left the restaurant, Pieter was beginning to wonder whether Yoshinori was the right kind of person to run such an important project.

The next morning, he decided to replace Yoshinori with Takashi – an MBA graduate (in his late twenties) from a top American university – who was working in a junior position on the project. Pieter spoke first to Yoshinori and then to Takashi. The former reacted to the news that he was to be moved sideways with extremely good grace. But, when Takashi was told about his promotion, he seemed both dejected and terrified. Over dinner that evening, a puzzled Pieter discussed Takashi's reaction with a close Japanese friend. His friend nodded wisely and said: 'The nail that sticks up will be hammered down.' Pieter frowned: 'What does that mean?' he asked. 'It's a well-known Japanese proverb', his friend replied. He then went on to explain that moving someone of Takashi's age so quickly and so publicly up the hierarchy was rather unusual. Takashi was probably embarrassed to be pushed forward in this way. And he would find it hard to earn the respect of his team members. Next day, much to Takashi's relief, Pieter reinstated Yoshinori as team leader.

If you come from an individualist culture like Pieter, you probably think it is perfectly normal to reward an individual's effort with public praise or rapid promotion. But, as his experience with Takashi shows, people from group-oriented cultures will often feel embarrassed to be treated differently from their peers.

Taking responsibility

Where you fall on the individualist—group-oriented scale will also affect your attitude towards taking responsibility.

A colleague of ours was running a workshop for a Japanese multi-national. The participants were all Europeans, apart from one Japanese guy called Makoto. The Europeans were given the opportunity to ask Makoto about aspects of Japanese culture that puzzled them. And Makoto was encouraged to ask similar questions of the Europeans. His first question was very revealing:

Why do Europeans always make excuses? And why do they never really say sorry?

The Europeans were incensed, and demanded examples. Makoto said:

If a European misses a deadline, he will say it was because there were bugs in the software, or a delivery didn't arrive. If a European has made a mistake, he will say it was because he was given the wrong figures, or the database hadn't been updated. These are excuses. Why doesn't he simply apologize? Or better, why doesn't he try and solve the problem?

The Europeans all argued that it was important to explain why a task had not been completed. From Makoto's perspective, however, they were simply blaming someone else for their own shortcomings. In Japan, people's responsibilities traditionally tended to be far less compartmentalized than in Europe. And, even today, the idea that *this is not my job* is still relatively uncommon. It doesn't matter what your job description is, if something needs to be done, you deal with it yourself.

Several years ago, Canning ran a course for some senior European managers from a well-known Japanese multinational. At the beginning of the course, one of the company's top Japanese managers gave the Europeans a 40-minute presentation explaining how he expected them to behave. Below is the text of one of the many slides he showed:

Take every responsibility. Never give excuses. Think only how to recover the situation. Forget your job description. Communicate with your manager frequently. You can perform your manager's job. Your manager's job is possibly your job. Do not refuse it because of job description. You are responsible for your subordinate's job. The job itself must be the aim of life.

Though many younger Japanese would say that this is now an old-fashioned view, most accept that it still exists inside a lot of their companies. And few Japanese would disagree with what this senior manager said next:

If somebody conflicts with others and is excluded from the community, he cannot survive. No prima donnas (people, like the main woman singer in an opera, who demand special treatment) are welcomed. No strong leaders are needed.

While leadership courses are now very popular in Japan, the Japanese definition of leadership is not the same as it is in, for example, the United Kingdom and the United States. Richard Pooley asked two British managers to draw a very simple picture that would illustrate their idea of leadership; he then asked two Japanese managers to do exactly the same thing. The results were fascinating. On both pictures, the leader was slightly larger than the team members. But the British had placed the leader to the far left of the page – in other words, *in front* of the team – and he or she seemed to be waving the team members forward, like an officer with a group of soldiers. The Japanese, on the other hand, had placed the leader to the far right of the page – in other words, *behind* the team – and he or she seemed to be trying to persuade the team members to 'go forward' to the left of the page. When asked to explain their pictures, the British managers talked about *leading by example, arguing their case well* and *motivating by both praising and criticizing*. The Japanese managers, on the other hand, talked much more about *coaching* and *teaching*.

In a vertical culture that is also individualist, you might expect the boss to make the decision and hand it down. But Japan is a vertical and group-oriented culture where harmony must be preserved at all costs, and individualist leaders are not appreciated. Strategic or policy decisions are only taken after a long and thorough consultation process called *nemawashi*. During *nemawashi*, managers have a series of one-to-one consultations with their team members. These often take the form of informal chats in the bar or spontaneous conversations in the office. People discuss as many options as they can think of. All the implications are examined – time, money, people – and all the subtleties of face-saving are considered. So, by the time the decision is finally taken, everyone's commitment to it is guaranteed. The way in which more individualist cultures challenge and disagree with one another at so-called decision-making meetings comes as a terrible shock to most Japanese business people. For them, a round table meeting is just a formality – to *rubber stamp* (ratify) what has already been agreed during *nemawashi*.

Monitoring performance

How far do you expect your subordinates to work on their own initiative? And how closely do you expect your boss to monitor what you're doing?

Again, expectations can vary considerably from place to place, as Renate – a German businesswoman – found when she first moved to Paris to work for a French company:

> I had always assumed that most Western Europeans worked in a similar way. However, a few weeks into my first project, my new boss saw me in the corridor, drew me to one side and said: 'I don't seem to have received any weekly reports from you.' I replied: 'Well, no. There's nothing of any interest to tell you yet. I'm still doing the groundwork.' My boss gave a typical French shrug and said: 'But that's no reason not to write a report. This project is my responsibility and I need to have regular feedback from every member of the team. It's normal.' I was astonished. When you're running a project in Germany, your boss just lets you get on with it. You only write a report when you've got something to say.

A French boss isn't just the manager. He is *le responsable*. Everyone in the department and everything that happens there is his responsibility. Which is why Renate's boss felt the need to keep a close eye on what she was doing. This was very different from Germany where, as Renate said, your boss usually leaves you to work on your own initiative.

Expectations in Russia are different again, as a Russian woman (who worked in the Moscow office of a German chemicals company) explained to our colleague Krystina Mecner:

> One of our team members was a Russian guy called Pavel. We had worked together on a previous project, and I had always found him to be a hard worker. But on this new team, his performance started to deteriorate. Instead of doing his job, he spent a lot of time surfing the internet and writing personal e-mails. The trouble was, our German team leader, Helmut, trusted us to do our work with little supervision. I spoke to Pavel myself, but it didn't have any effect. So I decided to give Helmut some advice: 'In Russia, a manager needs to lead and control. If you don't monitor what people are doing several times a week, they will take advantage'. Unfortunately, Helmut chose to ignore my advice and it wasn't long before Lara, another colleague, started to follow Pavel's example. Helmut seemed unaware of the problem and made no attempt to change his management style. In the end, it was Pavel and Lara themselves who got sick of his lack of leadership and complained to head office in Germany. After an investigation, Helmut was sent home and replaced with a manager who monitored what we were doing. Everyone was much happier and our performance improved.

As we saw in Chapter 1, culture clashes can be particularly painful when HQ tries to impose its own cultural norm on all its subsidiaries. Many of the new management techniques that companies adopt to try to create some kind of competitive advantage originate in the United States. After all, it was the Americans who turned management into an academic discipline. But the United States, for the most part, has an individualist and hierarchically flat business culture. And some of their management strategies are simply not suited to more vertical societies:

> Sarah worked at the London HQ of an American investment bank. As HR manager, it was her job to ensure the smooth introduction of a new 360-degree appraisal system in all of the bank's offices in Europe. But the Spanish were refusing to play ball. While their managing director and HR manager both claimed to be in favour of the system, the other senior managers were not. Sarah had sent numerous e-mails to the two men suggesting ways in which the system could be implemented, and had also spoken to each of them several times on the phone. But their message was always the same: 'We agree that the system should be introduced. But our senior managers are resisting it strongly. They say it simply isn't right for Spain.'

A 360-degree appraisal means that your performance is assessed not only by people above you in the hierarchy, but also by your peers and subordinates. In some cases, the company's clients are also invited to submit their comments. So why did the Spanish find this idea so hard to accept? Well, Spain certainly has a strongly vertical business culture. But that's not the only reason. It's also because Spain would probably fall to the right of the following scale:

Acquired status	Given status
People should be judged on what they do, not who they are.	Other factors – such as family, class, nationality, race, education, age, sex, religion – should also be taken into account.

50	40	30	20	10	0	10	20	30	40	50

The idea that businesses should be run along meritocratic lines is becoming more and more common. So, at first sight, you may well place yourself to the left of this scale. But is that how you *really* feel, or how you believe you *ought* to feel? If you're a man in your fifties, for example, how happy would you be to report to a woman in her early thirties? If you're from a fairly mono-cultural society, how would you feel if your company appointed a foreigner as CEO? If you and most of your colleagues went to one of the top universities, how would you all react if the company recruited someone with no academic qualifications as your new boss? This scale probably raises more issues than you think.

In given status cultures, how fast you work your way up the hierarchy doesn't just depend on how well you perform. For the Spanish bankers in the situation above, age and gender were also important factors. In Spain, and other vertical/given status cultures, managers often treat their subordinates in a paternalistic way. They look after them much as a father looks after his son. Not only will they champion them for promotion or the best jobs, and protect them from intra-company disputes, but they will also advise them on personal matters.

How could a subordinate possibly be asked to anonymously appraise such a father figure's performance? The idea was completely incompatible with the Spanish managers' cultural values. Their attitude was quite clear: *I look after my employees and if they're not happy they will find some way to tell me – just as a son would tell his father.* And what about their daughters, you may well ask? Well, unfortunately for Sarah, many older Spanish men – brought up in the highly conservative years when Franco ruled the country – still find it difficult to accept that women should be treated as equals in the workplace. That's not to say a woman manager can't do business perfectly effectively in Spain or other paternalistic cultures. But she needs to be aware of their values and expectations and, if necessary, adapt her behaviour accordingly.

In Spain – and Italy, too – it's not unusual for a senior manager who has retired to retain considerable influence over the staff in the company he used to work for. Many Northern Europeans are surprised when they discover this. Sarah was no exception. But when, during an informal chat, the Spanish bank's HR manager suggested that their retired CEO might be able to help her, she was perfectly willing to try playing the game the Spanish way. She called the influential 65-year-old and arranged to have dinner with him. Naturally, she let him choose the restaurant and pay the bill. And, even though it went against her feminist principles, she dressed and behaved to charm. During the meal, they discussed a wide range of different topics, but none of them related directly to business. It wasn't until the coffee and liqueurs arrived that the retired CEO briefly mentioned the 360-degree appraisal system. He knew all about the problems Sarah had been having. But he was sure the managers would accept the idea once he had spoken to them. A few months later, Sarah was able to report that the Madrid office had agreed to implement the system provided it was modified to suit local conditions.

The highly sophisticated former CEO had obviously been able to suggest a compromise that would satisfy Head Office and suit the Spanish managers' leadership style. If Sarah had not been prepared to seek his help, the outcome might have been very different. Trying to impose an appraisal system that was designed by an acquired status culture on managers from a given status society can cause serious long-term damage to the relationship between head office and subsidiary – as a number of our clients have discovered.

Getting people to play ball

Wherever you come from, you're unlikely to have much respect for colleagues who embarrass you in front of others, betray a confidence, fail to do their fair share of the work, or break their word in some way. When they come from the same culture as you, at least you have some common point of reference to measure their behaviour against. Even so, it's not always easy to work out what their motives really are, or how far you can trust them. And when they're from a different country, it can be harder still:

An international company appointed two high potentials – Jean-Claude from France, and Toshiyuki from Japan – to run a project together. They seemed to get on well and, after much discussion, worked out a modus operandi and detailed schedule that they and their teams could agree to. Toshiyuki went back to Japan and submitted a written report, outlining what they had agreed, to his boss. A few days later, Jean-Claude had a brilliant idea. There was a much more efficient way of handling the project. Jean-Claude discussed the proposal with his French team and, before long, everyone concluded that it would work perfectly. A delighted Jean-Claude submitted a revised schedule to the French steering committee. He then called Toshiyuki:

Jean-Claude: I've got some good news. We've managed to streamline the schedule. I'll mail you the details in a

	minute. But, basically, it means we'll be able to complete the project a couple of months earlier than we thought.
Toshiyuki:	You've changed the schedule?
Jean-Claude:	Yes. I suddenly realized that if we split the teams into eight work groups rather than six, we could overlap phases two and three, and run phases five and six concurrently.
Toshiyuki:	You've changed the work groups?
Jean-Claude:	Yes. It's so simple, I don't know why we didn't think of it before.
Toshiyuki:	I see... But I told my boss that the schedule had been finalized. I've already submitted my report.
Jean-Claude:	Well, just tell him we've had a better idea.
Toshiyuki:	It will be very difficult for me to explain the changes to him.
Jean-Claude:	I don't see why. I mean, changing the schedule is going to save a lot of time and money. I'm sure he'll be very pleased.

The project went ahead, but the relationship between the Japanese and French teams deteriorated fast. Toshiyuki and his colleagues weren't openly obstructive, but Jean-Claude got the impression that they were somehow 'working to rule'. Before long, the project had fallen seriously behind schedule, and the group's HR director was asked to find out what was going wrong. He asked Canning to run a series of cross-cultural workshops. The first one was with the Japanese team. Our colleague, Nigel White, asked them to role play a few typical business situations and then discussed the various cultural issues that arose. During one of these discussions, Toshiyuki suddenly exploded: 'But that's just typical of the French! They never stick to an agreement. Jean-Claude changed the project schedule after I had submitted it to my boss. This is totally unacceptable. How can I ever trust him again?'

Jean-Claude certainly didn't cynically set out to *renege on* (break) an agreement, or to make Toshiyuki's life difficult. Quite the reverse. His motives were honourable, and he behaved in a way that his French colleagues would probably regard as normal. But his actions caused fatal damage to the relationship. Once again, it's all down to differing cultural values. From the Cartesian Jean-Claude's perspective, if there was a more efficient way of scheduling the project, then it was only logical to adopt it. For him, taking decisions like this is part of a manager's job. It's normal. How could anyone possibly object?

Well Toshiyuki could, and did. From his perspective, a final agreement had been made. In his consensus culture, managers don't behave in such an individualist way. Strategic and policy decisions are only taken after long and careful *nemawashi*. And if you want to change them, there has to be another equally thorough consultation process. When he changed the plans, Jean-Claude had not only broken his word. He had also put his Japanese colleague in an embarrassing position. Toshiyuki would lose face with his Japanese boss and probably with his Japanese team members too.

Jean-Claude was completely unaware of how Toshiyuki felt. He had learnt a lot about Japanese culture before joining the project team, and always made a genuine effort to see things from his Japanese colleagues' perspective. But, on this occasion and on this issue, it didn't even occur to him that there was a culture gap. Unfortunately, it's occasions like this that can present the greatest danger to the international business person. Stereotypes can be reinforced and relationships irrevocably damaged without your even realizing it.

Clearly, learning how your international colleagues expect to be treated and why takes time. And no matter how carefully you do your homework, there will always be some cultural gaps that you're not aware of. So does that mean misunderstandings of this sort are inevitable? Well, no. Not necessarily. It's all a question of how sensitively you communicate.

In fact, it was the way Jean-Claude communicated with Toshiyuki that caused most of the trouble. You see, he focused exclusively on himself and his own agenda. And, in our experience, that is a major cause of misunderstanding and conflict, not only between people from different cultures, but between compatriots too. No matter where you go in the world, you'll come across some people who seem to be natural born communicators. Everyone respects them; everyone likes dealing with them; everyone seems to be prepared to make an extra effort to help them. You can probably think of one or two of your own colleagues who fit this description. And if you analyse what these successful communicators do, you'll find that they have one thing in common. Whoever they're dealing with, whatever they're talking about, however committed they are to their own views and values, they show empathy with the other person.

Empathy is the ability to put yourself in someone else's position; to see the world through their eyes; to imagine how they're feeling. Clearly, the more you have in common with someone, the easier it is to show empathy. But if you want to be a successful international communicator, you have to develop the ability to empathize with everyone – even people who seem to look at the world from a completely different perspective.

The trouble is, if you try to work out *how* these people show empathy, you end up with a list of practices that are so obvious they sound simplistic: keep an open mind; find out how people feel and what kind of pressures they're under; imagine why they find it hard to accept your proposals; ask questions and really listen to the answers. All of this is plain common sense, isn't it? Well yes, it is. Unfortunately, when you're under stress, common sense can be one of the first things that goes out of the window. If you've got a deadline to meet and your colleagues are refusing to play ball with you, empathizing with their problems is often the last thing you feel like doing. And if, like Jean-Claude, you're totally convinced that your proposal is the right one, it may not even occur to you that Toshiyuki sees things differently. But if only Jean-Claude had used a bit of imagination, if only he had kept an open mind, asked a few perceptive questions, and really listened to what Toshiyuki was saying, the conversation might have gone very differently:

Jean-Claude: *I'm calling about the project schedule. I think I've found a way to save some time – and quite a bit of money too.*

Toshiyuki: Really? How?

Jean-Claude: *Well, if we split the teams into eight work groups rather than six, we could overlap phases two and three, and run phases five and six concurrently.*

Toshiyuki: Oh! Very big changes.

Jean-Claude: *Yes. It would mean reworking the whole schedule, I'm afraid. How would you feel about that?*

Toshiyuki: It would be very difficult for me.

Jean-Claude: *Difficult? In what way?*

Toshiyuki: I told my boss that the schedule had been finalized. I've already submitted a formal report.

Jean-Claude: *Right... What would he say if you told him we wanted to change it?*

Toshiyuki: It would be very difficult for me. Everyone has been consulted. The final schedule has been agreed.

Jean-Claude: *I see... Well, obviously I don't want to cause you any problems with your boss. But as I said, it would save the company a lot of time and money... What would you and your colleagues usually do in this kind of situation?*

This time, Jean-Claude had tried to put himself in Toshiyuki's position before he picked up the phone. Of course, given his cultural conditioning, it would have been hard for him to anticipate his Japanese colleague's reluctance to tell the boss that everything was going to be changed. But it didn't take much imagination or common sense to realize that Toshiyuki might not be very enthusiastic about revising the schedule. After all, they had just spent several weeks planning the project together. So Jean-Claude was careful not to present his colleague with a unilateral decision. Instead, he:

▨ made a **tentative proposal**

I think I've found a way to save some time – and quite a bit of money too.

▨ **acknowledged** that it would involve making substantial changes

It would mean reworking the whole schedule, I'm afraid.

▨ asked a **series of open questions** and really **listened** to the answers

How would you feel about that?

Difficult? In what way?

What would he say if you told him we wanted to change it?

What would you and your colleagues usually do in this kind of situation?

By showing empathy, Jean-Claude kept all the channels of communication open. As a result, at least he stands some chance of getting the schedule changed without damaging the relationship. Maybe Toshiyuki will suggest that Jean-Claude should ask the French boss to speak to the Japanese boss. Maybe he'll have some other proposal. Or perhaps he'll simply repeat that the whole situation is very difficult for him. It's anyone's guess. But whatever he does say, Jean-Claude is in a much stronger position than he was at the end of the first conversation. He now knows that this is a delicate issue, and that he and his French colleagues will have to think very carefully about the best way to handle it.

It's hardly rocket science, is it? And yet a lot of the international business people we work with (rocket scientists included) are frequently astonished at how much difference asking a few questions and showing a bit of empathy can make:

> An Italian lawyer, who had just started a one-year secondment with a law firm in London, came to Canning for a few days' one-to-one training. When James, her trainer, asked how she was getting on with her British colleagues, she said that she was finding it very difficult to make friends: 'I try to be friendly and converse with them, but they are very cold; very closed. It's always the same. After a few minutes, they find some excuse to bring the conversation to an end.'
>
> James was rather puzzled and suggested that they role play one of these conversations. The Italian woman agreed, and started talking... about herself. Ten minutes later, she was still talking. And she would probably have gone on a lot longer if James hadn't interrupted her. 'Why', he asked 'didn't you try to find out something about me?' The Italian woman said: 'In Italy, when you want to show that you are open and friendly, you do it by telling people a lot about yourself.' James explained that the reverse was true in the United Kingdom: 'If you want to make friends with your colleagues here, you need to show interest in them. And that means asking questions.' The Italian woman looked doubtful, but agreed to try to follow his advice when she got back to her office. A few weeks later, she called James: 'You were right. Asking questions has really broken the ice. I've now made friends with several of the women in the office. And the other day they invited me to join them for dinner.'

It isn't only *countries* that have their own way of looking at the world, and their own way of doing things. Different professional groups have their own 'culture' too. It's a question of who or what you identify with. An American medical doctor, for example, may feel she has more in common with a doctor from Syria than she does with the administrators in her own hospital. Inside every company there are always certain groups or individuals who seem to look at things from completely opposing perspectives:

Financial control: *You're obviously going to have to cut your direct costs. Otherwise there's no way you're going to meet the profit target.*

Profit centre: Quite frankly I'm not even prepared to discuss my direct costs until you can justify the HQ charges we had to pay last year.

Financial control:	It's simple enough. Untracked costs have to be paid for by the profit centres. They're allocated on the basis of headcount, office space and the volume of tracked costs. How else can we work it out?
Profit centre:	Good question. How else could we work it out? And, more to the point, what steps are you taking to bring your own costs down?

It's a familiar situation, isn't it? These two colleagues come from the same national and corporate culture. They know their place in the hierarchy, who's responsible for what and how people expect to be treated. But there's still a 'culture' gap between them. The financial controller is one of the *cops* (policemen); one of the people – accountants, auditors, compliance officers, quality control executives, HR managers even – whose job it is to make sure that everyone follows the rules, and that overall corporate objectives are achieved. The profit centre manager, on the other hand, is one of the risk-takers – the people who go out into the market and bring back the business that pays everyone's salary. Clearly, both groups perform a vital role. The company couldn't survive without either of them. But the nature of their jobs means that they often find it hard to identify with each other.

The trouble is, they're never going to bridge this 'culture' gap if each of them persists in focusing exclusively on himself and his own agenda. Take the financial controller, for example. He went to the meeting with a specific message to deliver: *You've got to meet the profitability target. And to do that, you'll have to cut your direct costs.* Which may be perfectly true. But the profit centre manager went to the meeting with an equally specific and clear message to deliver: *The HQ charges we had to pay last year were unacceptably high. If you don't reduce your costs, we won't meet our profitability target.* They started out on opposite sides and they stayed there.

Of course, there may not be any alternative to cutting the profit centre's direct costs and, if so, the financial controller will need to *show steel* (be firm); at the same time, the profit centre manager will certainly want to communicate his dissatisfaction with the HQ charging system and demand adjustments to it. But that doesn't mean the conversation has to turn into a battle. Instead of starting off with: *You're obviously going to have to cut your direct costs. Otherwise there's no way you're going to meet the profit target*, the financial controller could have:

▓ asked an **open** question – one that starts with *who, what, why, where, how*;

- really **listened** to the answer;

- **acknowledged** the profit centre manager's difficulties and shown genuine **empathy** with him;

- probed the profit centre manager's attitude to cutting his direct costs with a **closed** question – one that invites a *Yes* or *No* answer;

- **answered** his concerns calmly and reasonably.

If he had, the conversation might have gone very differently:

Financial control:	*How do you feel about the new profitability target?* (**open question**)
Profit centre:	I don't think we stand any chance of achieving it, to be honest. I mean, we're still trying to build up the market.
Financial control:	*Yes, I can see that it's going to be much harder for you than for the more established units.* (**empathy**) *But your headcount is quite high in relation to turnover. Do you see any scope for cuts there?* (**closed question**)
Profit centre:	To be honest, laying off a couple of people isn't going to make much difference. My major problem is the HQ charge. It accounted for nearly 30 per cent of our total operating costs last year. I mean, that can't be right, can it?
Financial control:	*Well, I'm sure we've only charged for the services you used. But 30 per cent is very high, I agree.* (**answer**) *Why don't we go through the figures together and see if we can work out where...*

This approach won't guarantee success. But at least the two colleagues are listening to each other. At least they are trying to understand one another's point of view. And that has to be better for the relationship than talking at each other from behind well-established battle lines.

Summary

Once you step outside your own corporate and national culture, you'll find people whose attitudes towards power and authority are very different from your own. And if you measure the way they behave against your norms, you could end up misinterpreting their motives: a Brit would probably suspect his French colleagues of duplicity if they went behind his back to the boss; a French *responsable* might think his German subordinate was trying to cover something up if she failed to report back to him regularly; and a Japanese manager might think his European counterpart was being a prima donna if he made a policy change without consultation. The modern business world is complex, diverse and often stressful.

And there's no panacea that will magically cure all these communication problems. But if you try to show a bit of genuine empathy you'll find that, at the very least, it can be an effective painkiller. So remember:

■ ask plenty of **open** questions – ones that start with who, what, why, where, how;

■ really **listen** to the answers;

■ probe for more information by asking **closed** questions – ones that invite a Yes or No answer;

■ **acknowledge** the other person's position;

■ **answer** their concerns calmly and reasonably.

3 Knowing the limits

What is wanted is not the will to believe, but the will to find out, which is the exact opposite.

(Bertrand Russell, *Sceptical Essays*, 1928)

It's easy to see why you need to try to adapt to the way your international partners interpret the party line or handle the hierarchy. But what can you do when you come up against beliefs or practices that seem to go against everything that you believe to be right?

People who cynically set out to break the law, or behave in a way that they know is morally reprehensible exist in every culture:

When an accountant in a subsidiary presented the annual report she had prepared, the parent company CFO said: 'You'll have to rework these figures. The bottom line is four million below the number we want.' 'Reworking' the figures to produce the bottom line the CFO wanted would have meant deliberately disobeying accountancy conventions and breaking the law. So the accountant refused. Several weeks later, the company made her redundant. As she didn't want to get involved in a lengthy and possibly career-damaging court case, she decided not to take any further action.

A sales manager was sent by his company to an emerging market country to negotiate an important contract. On the first evening, his hosts took him out to dinner and kept refilling his glass with wine and liquor. The sales manager got very drunk. So much so, that when he was invited to spend the night with one of the four beautiful girls who had suddenly appeared on the scene, he acted completely out of character and accepted the offer. Next morning, his hosts presented him with the contract and asked him to sign it. 'But we haven't negotiated the terms', said the sales manager. 'Yes we have', said his hosts. 'The negotiation took place last night. Don't you remember?' When he still refused to sign, his hosts started to threaten him. After an extremely uncomfortable half hour, the sales manager eventually managed to leave without signing anything. When he got back home, he overcame his embarrassment and told his bosses exactly what had happened. He then phoned the prospective partners and arranged to meet them on neutral territory to negotiate the deal. He went to the next meeting with two colleagues and, this time, none of them drank anything stronger than mineral water.

By anyone's standards, presumably even by their own, the CFO and the 'negotiators' in these two situations were doing the wrong thing. In deciding how best to deal with them, all our two business people could do was follow their own conscience. The accountant refused to break the law; on the other hand, she wasn't prepared to take the company to court for fear of damaging her long-term career prospects. The sales manager was stupid to get drunk, and even stupider to accept the offer of sexual favours. But he followed his conscience once he *had sobered up* (was no longer drunk) – even though telling his bosses what had happened must have been embarrassing, and could even have lost him his job.

Though there's plenty of malpractice in the world, there's plenty of honourable conduct too. The advice below is as relevant today as it has ever been:

Exercise caution in your business affairs, for the world is full of trickery. But let not this blind you to what virtue there is; many persons strive for high ideals, and everywhere life is full of heroism.

(Max Ehrmann, *Desiderata*, 1927)

On home ground, you will have a pretty good idea of what you should or shouldn't do; and you will usually be able to distinguish between those who are *resorting to trickery* (being deliberately dishonest) and those who are trying to be virtuous. But when you're dealing with people from different cultures, it's not always easy to work out whether they're overstepping the limits of what their society regards as acceptable behaviour or not. That's because no two cultures draw the line between what is right and what is wrong in exactly the same place.

Some may believe that rules, regulations and the laws of the land should be followed *to the letter* (literally), whatever the circumstances; while for others, there are situations where bending the rules, or finding ways round complex and seemingly senseless legislation, is perfectly acceptable. What one person regards as a gift, another may see as a bribe. One culture's idea of fair competition may be perceived elsewhere as sharp practice. Your attempts to be discreet may be interpreted by some as dishonesty.

Rules, regulations and the laws of the land

Where do you stand on bending the rules?

Fixed truth						Relative truth				
There are clear rights and wrongs.						What is right and wrong depends on the circumstances.				
50	40	30	20	10	0	10	20	30	40	50

Whether you believe rules should be followed to the letter, or interpreted according to the circumstances, you will find that not everyone shares your view:

Thomas, a Swiss businessman who had just moved to Italy, needed some legal advice. Gianni, an Italian friend, gave him the name of a good lawyer in a reputable firm. 'He's not a partner,' said Gianni, 'but he's very competent, and he won't overcharge you.' Though the firm's hourly rate was, in fact, fairly high, Thomas was very impressed with the young Italian who welcomed him into his office the following day, and decided to engage his services.

The matter was quickly resolved and Thomas asked the lawyer what the final bill was, and how soon he would receive it. The lawyer said: 'Well, that depends on how you want to pay; and, of course, on whether you require an invoice.' Thomas looked puzzled. 'It's up to you, of course,' the Italian added. 'But a cash payment would save you quite a lot of money.' Thomas had heard that plumbers, electricians and even hairdressers in Italy sometimes asked for cash to avoid paying value added tax. But he couldn't believe that a firm of lawyers would be prepared to break the law in this way. His response was instinctive: 'I'd like an official invoice, please.'

When he left the lawyer's office, he called Gianni and told him what had happened. His friend was rather surprised: 'But why did you do that?' he asked. 'You could have saved yourself some money, and helped the lawyer to supplement his income. Non-partners don't earn very much, you know.' It was only then that Thomas realized that the lawyer would have kept the money for himself. 'But that's completely illegal', he said. 'Well, technically, I suppose it is', replied Gianni. 'But everyone does it. I mean, what harm does it do?'

Thomas clearly comes from a fixed truth culture where rules are supposed to be followed to the letter, whatever the circumstances. People from North America, Australia, and northern Europe tend to lean this way. Gianni, on the other hand, comes from a relative truth culture where the circumstances dictate the way you behave. He gives his loyalty to his family and the people he is close to rather than to a set of abstract rules. People from much of South/South-East/East Asia, Africa and around the Mediterranean tend to lean this way. And when someone from a fixed truth culture comes up against someone from a relative truth culture, they may well have trouble interpreting one another's motives.

Before Thomas jumps to the conclusion that Gianni and his lawyer friend are law-breakers and cheats who have no moral code, he should pause for a moment and ask himself what lies behind their attitudes and behaviour. Similarly, Gianni should ask himself what makes Thomas react in what seems, to him, such a rigid and unimaginative way.

Where Thomas comes from, people tend to have faith in the State. Switzerland is famous for actively involving all of its citizens in the democratic and lawmaking process. Honest, upstanding citizens who have faith in the way their society is governed, and who believe their judicial system is transparent and fair, tend to regard obeying the laws of their land as a moral duty. The limits are very clearly defined: for example, paying taxes is right; evading them is wrong.

Gianni, on the other hand, has little faith in the State. Indeed, he has developed a fairly cynical attitude towards it. In any case, Italian legislation is so complex, and the bureaucracy so labyrinthine, that Gianni would find it difficult to follow laws and procedures to the letter even if he tried. So he's a pragmatist. He has to be. If he weren't, the excessive regulation he lives with would paralyse him. What his lawyer friend suggested is certainly *illegal*. But to Gianni's mind, it is not *immoral*. The fact that he sees nothing particularly wrong with breaking certain laws does not mean that he has no moral code. Far from it. In his personal relationships he demonstrates a very high level of loyalty and integrity. He genuinely wanted to help both his Swiss friend to save some money and his lawyer friend to supplement his income. The partners of the law firm earn huge salaries. So where's the harm in redirecting a little of their income to a more deserving cause? It's quite possible, in any case, that the partners are aware of what their more junior colleagues are doing, and have pragmatically chosen to ignore it.

No one can expect Thomas to do something that he regards as morally wrong. But, equally, he will find it hard to do business successfully in a relative truth culture like Italy if he immediately jumps to the conclusion that Gianni and his lawyer friend have no moral values. And when Gianni does business with people from a fixed truth culture, he may well have to modify his highly pragmatic approach. If not, there's a danger it will undermine his business partners' confidence in his integrity.

Whatever kind of moral dilemma you're confronted with, the golden rule is to try to evaluate the situation as calmly and objectively as possible:

When a large German company set up a plant in China, they sent Klaus – an experienced manager in one of their home plants – over there to run it. One Sunday, a couple of years later, Klaus was doing some work on a report for HQ when he realized he had left a disk he needed in his office at the plant. He decided to go and pick it up. As he was about to leave, he heard noises coming from the factory. No one worked on a Sunday, so he thought he had better investigate. He could hardly believe his eyes: one of the production teams was running a line. What they were doing was obviously 'unofficial', but Klaus was careful not to overreact. He simply shouted a warm greeting to Mr Li (the foreman), said he needed to see him on Monday morning, and then discreetly left for home.

Next day, Mr Li told him the truth: 'We were just trying to earn a little extra income', he said. 'I really am very sorry. But we were only using the line; we brought in all our own materials from outside.' Klaus knew that Mr Li was very well connected with local politicians. So, again, he was careful not to overreact. He simply explained that the machines had a specific 'MTBF' (Mean Time Between Failure) and that they were depreciated on that basis. Mr Li thought for a moment and then made a suggestion that would get round the problem: he and his team could pay the company a hire charge for the use of the line.

Though this was highly irregular, Klaus decided to accept his proposal. The result was a very motivated workforce and a very co-operative Mr Li. Unfortunately, the 'income' had to be recorded in the accounts, and it wasn't long before German HQ asked Klaus for clarification. Klaus tried to explain the reason for his decision and the benefits it had produced; but the CFO refused to listen and insisted that Klaus put a stop to the unofficial production immediately.

Two weeks later, the local safety standards officer paid a surprise visit to Klaus's plant. He produced questionable evidence that they were in breach of certain safety regulations and closed the plant down. It remained closed for six weeks. When it reopened, the workforce never regained their previous levels of effort and motivation.

Who do you sympathize with here? The entrepreneurial, but seemingly underhand, Mr Li? The highly principled, but obviously dogmatic, CFO? Or the pragmatic, but possibly too liberal, Klaus? Once again, your answer will depend, to some extent, on how comfortable you personally feel about bending the rules to suit the circumstances.

The Chinese production team certainly knew that what they were doing was highly irregular. But did they think it was immoral or illegal? Did they think anyone was going to suffer, or lose out, as a result of their actions? If you consider the norms and attitudes that are prevalent in Chinese society, you would probably conclude that they did not. But what about the safety standards officer? Was it Mr Li who called him in? And if he did, what were his motives? No one can know for sure, but Mr Li was very well connected with local politicians.

The fact is, despite recent changes in the fast-developing areas around cities like Shanghai and Guangzhou, China is still largely a vertical, paternalistic, Confucian society. Mr Li's business world is intensely personal and closely linked to the extended circle of family and friends who are at the centre of his universe. The members of this extended circle have a strong sense of duty and responsibility towards one another and will always be willing to exchange favours. And Mr Li will try to achieve as much as possible through these *guanxi* (connections). In all his dealings with them, he will practise the art of *mian zi* (giving face). That means doing everything he can to make the other person feel good, and trying to avoid conflict wherever possible.

Personal connections are also used to obtain goods and services that would not be available on the open market. *Zhou houmen* (literally, going through the back door) has become common practice. This unofficial economy far exceeds most black markets in its size and complexity. Recent history has taught Mr Li to live for today; to take a practical, short-term approach. So it's not surprising that he and the production team were quick to seize this golden opportunity to make a bit of extra money on the side. After all, what harm would it do? They weren't stealing the company's materials. And once they knew about the MTBF problem, they were perfectly willing to pay for the use of the line.

So was Klaus right to legitimize this unofficial operation? That depends on your point of view. From the CFO's perspective, appropriating company property for private use was unquestionably wrong. By giving in to Mr Li, Klaus may have made his own life easier in the short term. But he had given entirely the wrong signal to the Chinese workforce: here was a manager they could manipulate. In the long term, showing that he was prepared to bend the rules could have disastrous consequences. To us, as Brits, on the other hand, it seems that everyone would gain by Klaus's creative compromise. But then the British tend to have a fairly deregulated mentality; as long as people play fair, who cares about the rules?

Whether Klaus's decision was right or wrong is a matter of opinion. But there's no denying that the way he reacted on that Sunday afternoon, and his behaviour towards Mr Li the following day, were absolutely right. During his two years in China, Klaus had learnt a lot about the local culture. He knew all about *connections*, *giving face* and *going through the back door*. So he wasn't in the least surprised that Mr Li had not told him about their unofficial operation. The Chinese team had often withheld information from him in the past. Indeed, to save face and maintain harmony, they usually said very little about problems or irregularities. Instead, they tried to present him with as positive a picture as possible of what was going on. Klaus knew that to manage his Chinese team effectively he needed to invest plenty of time and effort in getting to know them, and earning their trust. And, perhaps most importantly, he had learnt that if he wanted to gain their cooperation, he needed to modify the frank, direct and explicit communication style that came naturally to him and his German colleagues.

So, on that Sunday afternoon, Klaus was very careful to avoid a direct confrontation with Mr Li. Of course, he was shocked to see what was going on. But he didn't show it. He remained calm, greeted Mr Li courteously, and discreetly told him that he needed to see him the following day. The next morning, he maintained a constructive and positive attitude. He didn't pass judgement on Mr Li's actions. Instead, he patiently told him about the MTBF problem. Given this firm but fair approach, if Klaus had decided to stop the unofficial production there and then, we believe he could have done so without damaging the relationship.

Back home in Germany, Klaus would most probably have taken the same view as the CFO. But he wasn't back home. He was in China managing a team whose attitudes and beliefs were different from his. So he did everything he could to try to bridge the culture gap. If you find yourself in a similar position to Klaus, we recommend that you follow his example:

- don't overreact or pass hasty judgements;

- keep an open mind;

- ask yourself why you think what's happening is wrong; and why the people you're dealing with draw the line in a different place;

- re-examine the situation as objectively as possible;

- look for ways of resolving it that will be acceptable to both parties' moral values and beliefs;

- remain calm and constructive at all times.

Having gone through this process, Klaus decided that he could accept Mr Li's proposal to pay a hire charge for the use of the line without compromising his own, or indeed the company's, moral beliefs. And if the CFO had not withdrawn the privilege, the Chinese workforce would most probably have continued to repay their German boss's flexibility and fairness with continued cooperation and productivity. Of course, if you had been in Klaus's position, you might well have made a different decision. Which is fine. No one can expect you to condone something that you believe to be wrong. Whatever the situation, you have to remain true to yourself.

Gifts, favours and bribes

Bending the rules is one thing. But how comfortable do you feel about exchanging gifts and favours with the people you're doing business with?

Your answer will, to some extent, depend on where you fall on the following scale:

Functional						Personal				
We need to focus on business first and personal relationships later in order to do successful business.						We need to build a personal relationship first in order to do successful business.				
50	40	30	20	10	0	10	20	30	40	50

In cultures where business is personal, gift-giving and exchanging favours tend to be commonplace. After all, what better way of developing goodwill and demonstrating your wish to keep the relationship going? The problem is, where do you draw the line between a gift and a bribe? How do you distinguish between reasonable business entertainment and thinly disguised corruption? How do you identify the point at which doing someone a favour becomes sharp practice? Following the many corruption scandals that have been reported in the press in recent years, the world's leading multinational companies are being forced to give these questions some careful thought.

And some of them – particularly those in Northern Europe – are now so anxious to avoid any hint of corruption that they won't even allow their employees to pay for a business associate's dinner; or, indeed, to accept a meal. And even in Japan – a relative truth culture, where business is personal – a number of leading companies have now banned the traditional, twice-yearly exchange of gifts. Until recently, most Japanese business people presented beautifully wrapped gifts to a whole network of business associates during the official summer (o-*chugen*) and winter (o-*seibo*) gift-giving seasons.

International, national and individual beliefs do evolve, and behaviours do change. But it's a very slow process. Some Japanese companies may have banned the traditional gift-giving, but that doesn't necessarily mean they have suddenly come to the conclusion that this age-old custom is wrong or corrupt. Perhaps they're simply adapting to the way their US and Northern European partners behave. Or maybe they just see it as a convenient way of cutting costs without losing face.

Why some companies in the United States and Northern Europe have banned business entertainment is perhaps a little easier to understand. Few people would see anything wrong with taking a client out to dinner in a reasonably priced restaurant once every six months or so. But there are many who would think that inviting an overseas official and his wife for an all-expenses-paid trip to New York, Zurich or London was in the same category as bribery. As there are many grey areas between these two extremes, it's hard to establish clear-cut rules about what constitutes acceptable business entertainment and what does not. For people from a fixed truth culture, it's far easier simply to ban entertainment altogether. That way, the rule is absolutely clear and everyone can follow it to the letter.

It can be a little more difficult for companies to provide such clear-cut rules to their overseas managers who are struggling to deal effectively with local officials:

A French engineering company decided to move their plant in Indonesia to an area that was at lower risk of tsunami. The largest, heaviest and most expensive items were two transformers. Each was loaded onto a separate truck and the two drivers started the journey over the mountains of Java. But they never reached their destination. At some stage during the trip, the trucks had disappeared. The police – whom the company contacted straight away – were very sympathetic and promised to put all their resources on the case. 'But,' the police chief said, 'we do ask for your understanding as we're very short of funds and our resources are extremely limited. In fact,' he added 'we don't even have enough funds to keep our local Police Training School open.' One of the French managers had been in Indonesia for many years and he suspected that the police chief's body language was sending them a very clear message. So, after the meeting, he strongly recommended to his boss that the company should make a significant contribution to the Police Training School fund. Two days after they had made the donation, the two trucks with their transformers were found and restored to their owners.

Well, what do you think? Was the donation an acceptable way of persuading the police to do everything in their power to find the equipment? Or was it a bribe? Did the French respond objectively and flexibly to local expectations? Or did they compromise their moral values?

According to the British personnel manager of a large multinational's subsidiary in East Africa, paying money to anyone is a serious mistake:

Building a relationship with local officials is one thing; paying bribes is quite another. Our policy is absolutely clear: we never, ever pay money to anyone; and we never offer anything in return for a contract. But to build the relationship, we do offer help and, occasionally, small presents. For example, one of the ministers wanted to send his son to a public (fee-paying) school in the United Kingdom. I wrote a letter on his behalf to a headmaster I knew. Sending small birthday presents to an official's children is another good way of building a warm relationship: it means a lot to them that we know how old their children are.

Fortunately, small acts of kindness that demonstrate empathy and concern can often do as much, if not more, for a relationship than cash payments, expensive gifts or nights out on the town. When a French manager at Renault (let's call him Yves) saw that one of his Japanese colleagues from Nissan (we'll refer to him as Hideki) was in an embarrassing situation, he didn't hesitate to offer him some highly practical assistance. It was in the first few years of the alliance between these two companies, when their managers were still learning about one another's cultures and how best to bridge the gap between them. The impact of Yves' spontaneous act of kindness took the members of both companies by surprise:

On the first morning of a two-day meeting in Paris, Yves noticed that every time Hideki stood up, he kept self-consciously pulling his trousers up. Yves took him discreetly to one side at the coffee break. 'I see you're having problems with your trousers', he whispered. 'Yes', said Hideki. 'I forgot to pack my belt.' Without a moment's hesitation, Yves took his own belt off and handed it to Hideki: 'Here you are', he said. 'You can borrow mine. I don't need it.' Hideki quietly thanked him and unobtrusively put the belt on straight away. When he returned to Tokyo, he sent the belt back to Yves with a warm letter of thanks. From that moment on, relations between the two men and their teams improved beyond recognition. News of Yves' generous act spread to other departments in Nissan. And those managers who tended to think these *gaijin* (foreigners) were cold and unfriendly started to look at their French colleagues through different eyes.

The message is clear: however different their cultural values may be, your international business associates are human beings with the same basic needs and emotions as you. And so, sometimes, even the smallest of favours can have an unexpectedly dramatic effect.

Of course, there will be times when someone offers *you* a gift or entertainment. As we've already seen, some US and Northern European companies have banned their employees from accepting either. Many multinationals, however, take a slightly more pragmatic approach. An American IT company we know of helps its staff distinguish between gifts and bribes by offering the following advice:

Don't accept anything that can't be consumed in a day.

So the occasional business dinner is OK; a weekend in the Bahamas is not. You can accept a bottle of whisky with an easy conscience; but if someone gives you a case of whisky, you'll have to send it back.

Nepotism

Some cultures put nepotism in more or less the same category as corruption. Others regard giving jobs or contracts to members of their family, or clan, as a perfectly normal, logical and acceptable thing to do. On the status scale we looked at in Chapter 2, the former would probably lean towards the left; the latter to the right:

Acquired status	Given status
People should be judged on what they do, not who they are.	Other factors – such as family, class, nationality, race, education, age, sex, religion – should also be taken into account.

50	40	30	20	10	0	10	20	30	40	50

And when people from opposite ends of this scale meet, they're often genuinely puzzled by one another's attitudes:

A Swedish company had established very clear global purchasing guidelines: no more than 30 per cent of any particular item could be supplied by one vendor; quotes had to be obtained from at least three different suppliers; and contracts were to be awarded purely on the basis of price, delivery terms, reliability and quality. Anders, the Swedish regional manager for South-East Asia, was disturbed to note that, despite several reminders, the subsidiary in Vietnam did not appear to be following these guidelines. In fact, the range of suppliers they used seemed to be very limited, and most of them were Chinese. The subsidiary's Chinese manager seemed very unconcerned when Anders raised this problem with him. 'Well, of course most of our suppliers are Chinese', he said. 'I only use vendors I'm related to.' Anders was shocked and remained silent for a moment. Then he calmly explained that this practice was against company guidelines. 'But why?' asked the Chinese manager. 'Because it's unethical and anti-competitive. We're not allowed to do it in Sweden, and we can't allow our subsidiaries to behave in this way.' It was the Chinese manager's turn to be shocked: 'But I can't see what the problem is', he said. 'My family are much more loyal and reliable than people I don't know. I can call them any time of day or night. They can't escape me. And, of course, they give me much better discounts. Surely you don't want me to use suppliers I don't trust.'

Anders raised and lowered his eyebrows, and remained silent. After some thought, he realized that there was a lot of sense in what the Chinese manager was saying. He felt sure that HQ in Stockholm would be happy as long as the Vietnam plant *appeared* to be sourcing supplies from a number of different vendors. So he and the Chinese manager agreed to create a number of 'shadow' companies for each supplier. That way, the names on the invoices would be different and it would look as if they were complying with the 30 per cent rule.

How do you feel about Anders' decision? Would you have done the same thing? Or would you have insisted that your Chinese colleague follow HQ guidelines? Anders would probably fall towards the acquired status end of the scale above; he may well also feel that rules and procedures should be followed to the letter. But when he was confronted with this moral dilemma, he followed the golden rules: he was careful not to overreact; he asked himself why he thought giving contracts to relatives was wrong; and why the Chinese manager thought it was not only right, but actually beneficial to the company; then he re-examined the situation as objectively as possible; and found a way of resolving it that was acceptable to himself, his company, and his Chinese colleague.

Anders was only prepared to accept this compromise because he could see that it was beneficial to the company. But there are occasions when family loyalties seem to be seriously disrupting efficiency and discipline:

Jon, an Englishman, was sent to Botswana to run his bank's main branch in Gaborone. All the other managers and staff were locals. During the first couple of months, Jon noticed that the members of the back-office team seemed to be taking a lot of unofficial leave. In most cases, they were asking for an official holiday on a Friday, and then calling the bank the following Monday to say they wouldn't be able to return to work until the Wednesday or Thursday. Jon asked Busang – the bright, well-educated young back-office manager – what was going on. Busang went through the timesheets with him and offered a number of explanations: 'This woman had to go to a family wedding; that man had to attend his nephew's circumcision ceremony; these two people had to go back to their village and help with the ploughing', and so on. 'But why didn't they return to work on the Monday?' Jon asked. Well because, apparently, they had missed the bus, or the journey had taken longer than they had expected. When Jon explained that these unofficial absences were damaging the bank's efficiency, Busang looked puzzled. 'But when someone's away, we always share their work between us', he said. Sensing that Busang was unwilling or unable to exercise his authority over the team, Jon decided to have a word with the bank's deputy manager.

As you have probably guessed, most of the employees in the back-office – and indeed the bank – were members of the same family or clan. When Jon said that this was unacceptable, the deputy manager reacted in a very similar way to the Chinese manager in Vietnam. Unlike Anders, however, Jon was convinced that allowing nepotism to flourish was not in the company's interests. Clearly, firing people at this stage wasn't an option. But Jon was able to use the deputy manager's argument to put a stop to the unofficial leave-taking: 'You said that relatives are easier to control than outsiders,' he pointed out, 'in which case, I expect you and all the departmental managers to exercise that control. This absenteeism is unacceptable and I'd like you to make sure that it stops right away. If it doesn't, people will lose their jobs.' Though the situation improved dramatically, Jon still felt very uncomfortable with the fact that most of his staff were related to each other. From that moment on, he took part in all recruitment interviews and made sure that candidates from outside the clan were given equal consideration.

Towards the end of his first year in Botswana, Jon was surprised to discover that the family relationships inside the bank could sometimes work in his favour:

Busang's own timekeeping had started to deteriorate and he was always complaining of being tired. On some occasions he arrived up to an hour late and often left early. Jon asked the deputy manager what he thought the reason was: 'Oh, he has a few problems at home; his children have been ill', he said, somewhat unconvincingly. 'I'll have a word with him.'

But Busang's performance didn't improve. In fact, it seemed to get even worse. One day he went out of the office very early and left an important job undone. Jon was furious. So furious, in fact, that – without naming names – he told his chauffeur what had happened during the drive home that evening. The chauffeur – a man in his late fifties – listened in silence. As he pulled up outside Jon's home, he turned to him and said: 'If you permit, Sir, I would like to tell you about my nephew. He works for our bank here in Gaborone. In fact, it was he who recommended me for this position as your driver. When our family realized he was a bright boy with a lot of potential, we all paid for his education. And now that he has a good job, of course, it's his duty to support anyone in the family who needs help. The problem is, he doesn't earn enough at the bank to meet all his obligations. So he's had to find a second job – just like a lot of young men in his position. For the last six months, he's been driving a taxi in the evenings.'

Jon thanked the driver for his help, and fixed a meeting with Busang. He handled it as sensitively as he could, but the general message was: 'I know what's been happening. I'll give you an x per cent salary increase, on condition that you give up the evening job.' The young manager obviously knew that his uncle had interceded on his behalf, and accepted the offer right away.

It would not necessarily occur to a manager from an acquired status culture that his chauffeur would be able to help him with a personnel problem. But, to the majority of the world's people, age brings wisdom; elders are always consulted and often obeyed – regardless of the job they do or the income they have at their disposal. Without the older man's intervention, Jon would probably never have found out why the back-office manager's performance had deteriorated so sharply. Nor would he have been able to work out how best to resolve the situation.

This European bank's employment contracts specifically banned staff from taking a second job. So why didn't Jon simply fire Busang? Well, because – as his chauffeur had explained – nearly all the well-educated young people in Botswana were in a similar position to the back-office manager. So any successor would find it equally difficult to meet their family obligations on the salary that went with the job. By showing empathy with Busang's position, Jon was able to propose a solution that was firm but fair: 'If you want to stay at the bank, you have to give up the second job; I realize you're having problems so I'll give you a salary increase.' Now that he understood how the family relationships worked, Jon was confident that the uncle would make sure Busang honoured the agreement.

Unlike Anders, Jon remained firmly convinced that giving jobs or contracts to family members was unequivocally wrong; he didn't accept Busang's claim that the bank's efficiency was unaffected by the unofficial leave-taking; and he couldn't allow him to carry on doing a second job. Even so, he was careful not to overreact. Instead of reprimanding Busang for his failure to control the team – which is what he would probably have done back home in the United Kingdom – Jon discussed the problem with someone who understood the local culture. And when his deputy manager argued that family members were easier to control than outsiders, he calmly and very reasonably insisted that the managers should exercise that control. Instead of issuing an official policy document that would have been incompatible with local cultural values, he quietly and pragmatically decided to take charge of the recruitment process himself. And instead of firing Busang for doing a second job, he showed empathy with the young man's position and offered him a firm but fair solution to his problems.

Discretion versus dishonesty

No examination of differing moral values would be complete without some reference to where you draw the line between discretion and dishonesty. Successful relationships in every culture are based on trust and mutual respect. And, most people would agree, it's virtually impossible to build trust if the other person thinks you're behaving dishonestly or telling outright lies. The trouble is, what one culture perceives to be an outright lie, another may regard as discretion or even honourable behaviour:

When an Italian company wanted to export specialist food and beverage products to Japan, it sought the advice of a Dutch consultant who had lived and worked in the country for many years. He put them in touch with a local importer/distributor with whom he had done business on many previous occasions. With the Dutch consultant's help, the Japanese importer and Italian exporter reached agreement on sales volumes, batch sizes, delivery dates, payment terms and so on, and a deal was set up.

For 18 months, everything seemed to go according to plan. The Italians delivered the goods as agreed, and the Japanese settled their invoices in full and on time. As far as the Dutch consultant could see, however, none of the retail outlets which had been named by the Japanese distributor as major potential clients seemed to be carrying the Italian goods. The Japanese distributor offered the following explanation: 'Most of our current clients repackage the goods and sell them under their own name. But you should start seeing the Italian brand in the shops within a few months.'

When, several months later, there was still no sign of the Italian brand, the Dutchman was fairly sure something was seriously wrong. So he went to see his old Japanese friend and spoke frankly to him about his concerns. The Japanese distributor looked embarrassed, but was unable to offer a satisfactory explanation. At the end of the meeting, however, he invited the Dutchman to accompany him to the warehouse. As soon as they got there, the Dutchman realized what the problem was. The warehouse was full of Italian goods – many of them past their sell-by date. The distributor had not been selling anywhere near the volumes that had been agreed. But he hadn't felt able to admit this to his Dutch business partner.

If the Japanese distributor hadn't had such a strong relationship with the Dutchman, he would probably have cancelled the contract as soon as he realized there was little demand for the product. As it was, however, he felt a very strong *on* (personal obligation) to meet the targets that had been agreed. And he couldn't see any way of telling the Dutchman what was really going on without damaging their relationship and losing face. Indeed, his sense of obligation to the Dutchman was so strong that he was even prepared to endanger himself financially to honour it.

The Dutchman comes from a culture where people have been brought up to tell the truth, whatever the circumstances. Attitudes to the truth run very deep. So even though he had considerable experience of working in Japan, it still took him a while to understand what was going on. Someone with less experience of Japanese culture might have jumped to the conclusion that the distributor was being deliberately dishonest or duplicitous.

Of course, the Japanese distributor wasn't actually telling lies; he was withholding the truth. But what about the Romanian engineers in the situation below?

> A remote team of French and Romanian IT specialists were working on a joint project. The Romanians were responsible for developing and testing part of the software – a task that was scheduled to take six weeks. Every week, they sent a report to France saying that there were no faults and that they were on schedule. The French found this hard to believe and regularly called them to double check that everything was OK. But the message was always the same: 'No, there are no problems. Everything's going fine.' Well, the Romanians certainly completed the project on time. But the software they had produced was so full of bugs, the French couldn't even run it.

The Romanians must have known there were problems with the software. So why were they so reluctant to tell their French colleagues what was wrong and ask for their help? Well, like many former members of the Soviet Union, Romania is struggling to build its economy and establish its credentials in the new Europe. So maybe these Romanian engineers were worried that their colleagues in the French parent company would think they were somehow incompetent or technically inferior. Or maybe the communist era had taught them that admitting to mistakes could lead to severe reprisals. Whatever the reason, the French took the only sensible course of action, and sent one of their own managers over to Romania to lead and support the team.

Everyone withholds the truth to one degree or another, particularly when there's a need for discretion about company or personal matters. But, as our colleague Krystina learnt from a Russian woman she was training, you can't expect everyone to exercise the same degree of discretion over personal matters as you do:

> When I was working in Belgium, I made very good friends with the Spanish team members. In fact, I met them socially as well as at work, and I even told them one or two personal details and stories about myself. It didn't occur to me that they would repeat these confidences to other members of the team. But it wasn't long before I realized that this was exactly what they had done.

At around the same time, the Spanish team members were told, unofficially by a Spanish board member, that our German marketing manager was going to be promoted. Not only did they immediately pass the information on to everyone on the team, but they also expressed surprise and anger that the German guy hadn't told them about the promotion himself. Understandably, the German guy was furious that the Spanish board member hadn't waited for the official announcement.

As for me, I was horrified. The Spanish obviously couldn't be trusted. From then on, I avoided socializing with them and I never confided in them again.

In fact, the Russian woman told Krystina that she had, over time, come to understand why her Spanish colleagues had behaved in this way. It wasn't malice or lack of integrity. They weren't trying to embarrass or humiliate anyone. Quite the reverse. For them, it was important to share information with their fellow team members. *Sharing* information showed trust and concern; withholding it was a sign that people didn't trust each other.

Summary

As we saw at the beginning of this chapter, wherever you work in the world, you will occasionally come across people who are doing things which, by almost any standards, are deeply wrong. And when that happens, all you can do is follow your own conscience. Unless you are very unlucky, however, it's likely that most of the people you meet will be trying to do what their own culture regards as acceptable. It just seems wrong to you because you're looking at it from your own cultural standpoint.

When you're working internationally, navigating your way smoothly through the moral maze (labyrinth) will often require more time, more thought and more flexibility than it does at home. So remember the golden rules:

■ don't overreact or pass hasty judgements;

■ keep an open mind;

■ ask yourself why you think what's happening is wrong; and why the people you're dealing with draw the line in a different place;

- re-examine the situation as objectively as possible;

- look for ways of resolving it that will be acceptable to both parties' moral values and beliefs;

- remain calm and constructive at all times.

As the people in the situations we've looked at discovered, there's no room for casual assumptions or quick judgements. You may regard something as normal. But is it necessarily right? Is what the other person is doing really wrong? Or is it just unusual or irregular? Before you leap to any hasty conclusions about an international partner's moral probity, or lack of it, think carefully about your respective cultural assumptions. Once you know and understand your own limits and theirs, you should be able to work out how best to bridge the gap.

There will be some occasions when, like the Swiss businessman in Italy, you decide that you can't condone what the other person is doing. There will be others when, like the Swede in Vietnam, you decide that you can accept what's happening without compromising your moral principles. We would never suggest that you ignore your own sense of right and wrong. But if you look in the history books, you'll find plenty of examples of people – Galileo, to name but one – who were harshly punished for acts that were merely unusual, rather than wrong. Beware of falling into the same trap. Don't let an irrational fear of the unusual lead you to hasty decisions. And whatever decision you do reach, make every effort – as Klaus did with Mr Li – to treat people as they expect to be treated.

4 Knowing the form

Manners maketh man.

(William of Wykeham, 1324–1404, Motto of Winchester
College and New College, Oxford)

Most psychologists agree that human beings form an impression of one
another with lightning speed. This impression is based on innumerable
signals that neither person may be consciously aware of sending. When
you meet someone for the first time, you'll evaluate their general conduct
and interpret their eye, face and body language within minutes, if not
seconds. And as soon as the other person starts talking, you'll very quickly
reach a decision about what they're like: *hmm, honest, warm, full of fun –
this looks promising*; or *oh no, aggressive, arrogant, rude – I don't think
I'm going to enjoy working with this one*; and so on.

Good manners are all about showing warmth, consideration, deference
and respect to others. But the good manners you learnt at your mother's
knee go way beyond saying *please* and *thank you* or using the correct
form of address. Without realizing it, you also absorbed the *right* way to
use your eyes and body, the *right* things to say, the *right* way of saying
them, and the *right* time to say them. You know and instinctively follow
the form (socially acceptable behaviour). And when you meet people who
don't, you may well judge them negatively. The trouble is, what you
regard as good form may be considered very bad form somewhere else –
and vice versa.

Even when you're dealing with a culture whose social behaviours
appear similar to yours, you can't assume that they're exactly the same –
as a French rugby player found when he joined an English team:

> The English are not arrogant, just different. When I first came (to England), I
> wondered why nobody shook my hand when we met at the start of the day.
> I was hurt. But it is just the culture...
>
> (Thomas Castaignede, *Rugby World*, February 2003)

Business people all over the world shake hands with visitors when they arrive and when they leave. But the French (and a few other nationalities) also shake hands with everyone in the office every morning when they go into work. And, as a British friend of ours who was living in Paris soon discovered:

> People are unbelievably offended if you forget. They looked at me as if I had done something really obscene.

It seems that before Thomas arrived in the United Kingdom he already had some preconceptions that the English were *arrogant*. His teammates' failure to shake hands with him at the start of the day simply reinforced this stereotype. If he had stayed in the United Kingdom for only a week or two, he might have gone home convinced that the English were not just arrogant, but also cold and unfriendly. And he would probably have shared this view with his family and friends in France. That's often the way one nation's negative stereotypes of another are built up. It was only when Thomas had lived and worked among the English for a while that he realized they had the same impulse to be courteous and warm as any other nation. They just had a different way of showing it.

It's astonishing that such a minor difference in social form could create so much misunderstanding. But it happens all the time. There will always be some kind of gap between your social conventions and those of your international business partners. Finding out what the main differences are and making a conscious effort to honour local custom is relatively easy. Battling against your own subconscious can be much harder. In many respects, the way you relate to people is instinctive. And the way you interpret the signals they're sending is involuntary. Buried somewhere deep inside you is the belief that your own social form is universal. And before your conscious mind has time to remind you that these people come from a different culture, your subconscious has already interpreted their behaviour in the light of your own social norms – often unfavourably.

It's hard to build a warm and constructive business relationship with someone if your instincts have told you they're arrogant, rude, cold, dishonest or whatever. This chapter takes you through some of the areas in which social form differs from one culture to another. Our own experience has taught us that the more you know about the differences and the better you understand them, the easier it will be to overcome any negative judgements your subconscious mind may form.

Greeting people

We started with the apparently superficial question of when you shake hands with people. However, it's not just *when* you shake hands, but also *how* that sends different signals to different people. We asked three colleagues – A (male), B (male) and C (female) – to shake hands with a German, a Swiss, a Frenchman, a Frenchwoman, an Italian and a Brit. Colleague A gripped each person's hand very strongly indeed, B's grip was firm but not excessively so, C exerted no pressure at all with her hand. We then asked each person for their impressions:

A (male) – very firm grip

German and Swiss:

He had a good firm handshake. And he looked me straight in the eye. He seems very honest and straightforward.

Frenchman, Frenchwoman, Italian:

Ouch! He gripped my hand so firmly, he almost crushed my bones. People who do that are usually aggressive and pushy. My first impression is not favourable.

Brit:

Oh dear! This guy's going to be a real bore.

B (male) – firm but not excessive pressure

Italian:

His handshake was OK. But he didn't strike me as being a very warm person. He stood such a long way away from me.

Everyone else:

Good firm handshake. More or less what I would expect. Looked me in the eye. I wouldn't have any trouble trusting him.

C (female) – no pressure at all

German, Brit:

(recoiling in horror): Argh! That's horrible! I'd try to keep an open mind but that's given me a very bad first impression. I don't trust her. She's not my kind of person. And she stood right on top of me. I hate people who invade my personal space.

Swiss:

A lot of women have gentler handshakes than men. But, personally, I like a woman who grips my hand firmly. It shows they're strong and straight-forward. I wouldn't give this woman a job. She's got no spirit.

Frenchman, Frenchwoman, Italian:

It was softer than I would expect – even for a woman. If a man shook hands with me like that, I would think he was dishonest.

Of course these are very personal reactions and if you tried the same experiment with some other people from the same cultures, you might well get a different response. What's more interesting is the cultural conditioning that lies behind some of these comments. The Italian, for example, thought that B might not be a very warm person because *he stood such a long way away from me.* And the German and Brit thought that C was *invading their personal space* and it made them feel very uneasy.

One of the first things you absorb at your mother's knee is how comfortable people feel with physical contact and closeness. And, as our colleague Dr Jehad al Omari discovered, the form varies considerably from culture to culture:

When I first came to the United Kingdom as a student, I was struck by the lack of human interaction. I did some part-time work in a shop in Guildford. One day the female manager had a visit from another woman. Afterwards, she said the woman was her aunt. I found it hard to believe. No hugs, no kisses, nothing.

Where I come from, there's so much touching. As a child, you are handed from one lap to another. As a boy, you often carry one of your cousins or relatives around with you. You see Arab children whose cheeks are covered in red marks; they come from kissing. From the moment you are born, you're taught to express yourself physically as much as verbally. And it doesn't stop when you grow up. When you meet someone you have not seen for a while, you kiss – even one man to another.

During my first year at college in the United Kingdom, my Arab friends and I enjoyed shocking the British. We would kiss each other on both cheeks – just to see their reaction. It took some time for the joke to wear off. After I had lived in the United Kingdom for several years, I visited Jordan. I was walking along the street with one of my male cousins when he held my hand. My reflex action was to withdraw my hand immediately. I had not realized how British I had become! It took me a few minutes to remember that I was now at home and that it was perfectly normal for two men to hold hands. I took hold of my cousin's hand again. This was my first lesson in learning how to be at ease with both cultures.

Jehad obviously falls at the far right of the scale below:

Physically distant						Physically close				
I prefer people not to come too close to me physically.						I think physical closeness and touch are reassuring.				
50	40	30	20	10	0	10	20	30	40	50

The Italian in our handshaking experiment would lean towards the physically close end of the scale too. He told us, for example, that when he greeted his friends with a handshake, he would also squeeze their arm with his left hand. And if they were very close friends or family, he would find it quite natural to kiss them – men and women alike. The Brit and the German, on the other hand, would be likely to place themselves in the middle or slightly towards the physically distant end of the scale. If a man kissed either of them, or walked along the street holding their hand, they would probably feel extremely uncomfortable.

A while ago, Chris – the Welsh, rugby-playing co-writer of this book – worked for a week in London with a Turkish manager. As he said goodbye at the end of the course, the Turk gave Chris a perfectly normal (by British standards) handshake. A few weeks later, they met one another by chance in Istanbul. The Turk beamed with delight, rushed up to Chris, gave him a hug, and kissed him on the cheek. Despite the fact that Chris is an experienced cross-cultural trainer, his instinctive reaction was: *Help! Why's he kissing me? He never did that in London. This is really embarrassing.* After a few seconds, of course, he was able to overcome this subconscious reaction and analyse the situation objectively. In London, his Turkish friend had adapted his behaviour to suit British expectations. Now he was at home in Turkey, there was no reason why he shouldn't greet friends in the way that came naturally to him.

If it's up to the visitor to know and honour local customs, then presumably the next time Chris meets his Turkish friend in Istanbul, he should initiate the hugging and kissing himself. Well no, not if it makes him feel awkward and uncomfortable. He would only come across as clumsy or insincere. But he should be careful *not* to show surprise or embarrassment when his Turkish friend hugs him. And, of course, *not* to allow his own social conditioning to lead him to false or negative judgements.

Everyone who took part in our handshaking experiment said that they found it hard to trust people who didn't look them in the eye. But they were all European. To the Japanese and other Asian cultures, people who look you in the eye too directly and too long can appear aggressive and disrespectful. So if a German and a Japanese meet, should Klaus try to keep averting his gaze? And should Takashi force himself to stare non-stop into Klaus's eyes? Well, they should both make an effort to modify their behaviour slightly, of course. But you can't undo a lifetime's conditioning; you can't be expected to act in a way that makes you feel uncomfortable or unnatural. What you can do, however, is stop yourself from jumping to the wrong conclusions. Klaus isn't being aggressive or deliberately trying to behave disrespectfully; Takashi isn't being devious or dishonest. They're both trying to be courteous. They've just got different ways of showing it.

So where would you place yourself on the physically distant scale? If you're from an individualist culture (for example, the United States, the United Kingdom, Northern Europe), you will probably fall somewhere in the middle. But if you're from a group-oriented culture, you may well fall sharply towards one end of the scale or the other. Arabs, Africans, Indians, South Americans, Southern Italians and Greeks tend to be very tactile. With them, handshakes can go on forever, and they're likely to stand very close to you. In East and South-East Asia, on the other hand, people tend to be far more physically distant. In Japan, for example, physical contact between business people in the office is almost non-existent. Interestingly enough, however, when Japanese colleagues are socializing together in the bar after work, they seem to become more tactile and it's not unusual to see them touching one another on the arm or patting someone on the back.

While bowing rather than handshaking is the cultural norm, most Japanese businesspeople these days expect to shake hands with their foreign business associates. But it's worth remembering that, if you grip their hand too firmly, they could assume you're being aggressive. So if your natural handshake is very firm, you'll need to make a conscious effort to apply slightly less pressure when you're greeting your Japanese business partners.

Making small talk

So you've got through the introductions successfully. Regardless of how your business partners shook your hand, how directly they looked you in the eye, and how close they stood to you, you've kept an open mind about what they're like. Good. Now let's get down to the small talk. How long should it go on, do you think? Two minutes, five minutes, 10 minutes, 45 minutes? Ah, well, once again your answer will be influenced by what's considered good form where you come from. As we've already seen, some cultures prefer to focus on business first and personal relationships later; others feel the need to build a personal relationship before they can do business.

At the beginning of any meeting with someone from the Arab world, for example, people expect to spend plenty of time (45 minutes would not be unusual) getting to know one another, or cementing the relationship, and the conversation can extend to all aspects of life (family, hobbies, travel, current affairs, the economy, etc). And even when the business talk finally starts, people often continue to intersperse it with more small talk and pleasantries. In Japan, too, the aim at early meetings will be to develop personal trust. And while Takashi may not engage in social pleasantries for very long – especially if he's forced to do so in English or another foreign language – he'll probably expect to spend plenty of time exchanging information about your two companies before he's ready to discuss specific business proposals. In more functional cultures, on the other hand, people expect to start on the business agenda within minutes of sitting down. With Germans, Swiss, Scandinavians and Finns, for example, small talk is often no more than a couple of sentences.

So if the person you're meeting spends longer on small talk than you regard as normal, hide any irritation you may instinctively feel; and overcome any urge you may have to force the pace. Remember, it's unlikely that they're trying to annoy you or waste your time. They're simply following what their culture regards as good form. Similarly, if the other person launches straight into business without what you would regard as even the minimum of pleasantries, don't assume they're being deliberately cold or unwelcoming. They're probably just trying to be professional and businesslike – qualities that their culture puts a high value on.

Playing the conversation game

Of course, it's not just how long you spend on small talk that differs from culture to culture. The way you actually play the conversation game also sends signals that may be misinterpreted by your international business partners.

I once visited an Englishman, called Paul, who had been working in Germany for many years. He started telling me about his company. As he spoke, I interrupted him several times with comments and questions – in an interested and friendly way that would be considered quite normal in the United Kingdom and the United States. Paul began to look more and more annoyed. Finally, I realized why. I said, 'You don't like me interrupting you, do you, Paul?' He said, 'No, I find it really irritating. Quite rude, in fact.' He had been in Germany for so long that he was no longer used to the interactive way his compatriots discuss things. He expected me to let him finish before I took my turn.

The Englishwoman wasn't rudely or aggressively shouting Paul down, nor was she continually cutting across what he was saying. That would be considered bad form virtually everywhere. She was just showing a friendly and respectful interest. She was playing the conversation game according to the rules of her culture. Maybe if Paul had been German, she would have tried not to interrupt him. But he wasn't; he was a fellow Englishman, and so it took her a while to realize what the problem was.

Some cultures (the United Kingdom and the United States, for example) expect conversation to be fairly interactive. To them, interrupting with the odd relevant comment or question is good form. The Americans, for example, will often make comments in the affirmative that build on what the other person is saying, while the British tend to interact by asking questions. And when people from these two cultures are confronted with a business partner who sits and listens to them in absolute silence, it can make them feel uneasy. They may wonder if they have said something wrong, or even jump to the conclusion that the other person is cold or lacking in personality.

Other cultures (the Japanese and the Finns, for example) are used to waiting their turn to speak. For them, conversation is often like a series of mini-monologues. They're not used to being interrupted, and when they meet someone who expects to conduct a conversation in a more interactive way, their instincts may tell them that he or she is ill-mannered, disrespectful or superficial. Such cultures are often very comfortable with silence. It shows that you're thinking about what has been said. With them, rushing to fill the silence can send completely the wrong signal, as our colleague, Gary Walker, discovered on his first-ever sales trip to Finland:

The first guy I met was unbelievably *taciturn* (unwilling to converse). Everything I said was greeted with a long silence. To be honest, I thought there was something wrong with him – you know, some kind of personality disorder. Being a typical Brit, I believed at the time that everyone in the world could be charmed with a bit of smooth-talking. So, every time there was a silence, I filled it. This was a fatal mistake. I soon learned that the Finns actively mistrust people who are too effusive.

How do you instinctively play the conversation game? Your answer will, to some extent, depend on where you would place yourself on the scale below:

Reserved	Effusive
I think you should talk only when you have something relevant to say.	Lots of talk indicates warmth and interest. Silences should be avoided.

50   40   30   20   10   0   10   20   30   40   50

At the far left of the scale you would probably find the Finns, while people from the Arab world would be likely to place themselves at the far right. The British and Americans would probably lean towards the right, while the Germans and Swiss might well lean towards the left. Interestingly enough, though, while the Germans are not used to interrupting people mid-flow, they are not particularly comfortable with silence. In this respect, they are more similar to the British and Americans.

Choosing what to say and how to say it

You're bound to draw conclusions about what people are like from what they choose to say, and how they choose to say it. The trouble is, the way even the most basic and universal sentiments are expressed can vary considerably from culture to culture. Take saying *thank you*, for example. It's something every child learns to do from a very early age. And you'll find an equally short and simple equivalent – *merci, gracias, dankeschön, arigato* and so on – of these two 'important little words' in virtually every language. But that doesn't necessarily mean that the way your international colleagues instinctively express their gratitude will be the same as yours.

In cultures where there's a strong oral tradition, for example, the use of metaphors, poetic language and colourful turns of phrase are usually much admired. When Penny was working, a while ago, with a senior businessman from Saudi Arabia, he thanked her for a very simple piece of advice she offered him by saying: *These are jewels you are giving me. Really jewels. I am so grateful.* Using a metaphor to express his gratitude came perfectly naturally to him. That's because, from a young age, he had listened to his elders in the *majlis*. This is a large room in which the men of the tribe regularly gather together to discuss family affairs and to socialize. Though the name of the room varies from place to place (for example: *madeef* in Syria and Iraq, *madafa* in Jordan, *diwanihey* in Kuwait), these gatherings are commonplace throughout the Arab world. And it's there that young boys sit with the men and learn the art of conversation and storytelling. Good raconteurs are much admired so naturally the boys are keen to memorize the stories that are told and to imitate the metaphors and colourful language that is used.

In other parts of the world – much of Northern Europe, for example – people tend to express themselves more plainly and simply. During a recent one-week intensive language course, one of the group members – a German – had to take a morning off to attend a meeting. Naturally our colleague was anxious to help him catch up with the rest of the group. So she spent her lunch break typing up a summary of everything he had missed. When she handed the notes to him after lunch, he simply said: *Thank you.* To him, this was a perfectly normal and well-mannered response. But someone from a culture where people express themselves more effusively and colourfully might well have found it rather terse, and even have concluded – quite wrongly – that the German was cold or ungrateful. And, of course, the kind of language the Saudi Arabian used might well make a plain-speaking Northern European feel uncomfortable or even suspicious of the other person's motives.

So even something as simple as the way you choose to say *thank you* can be open to misinterpretation. That's why documents that have been translated from another language sometimes sound strange or even slightly comical. You see, it isn't just a question of converting the actual words or phrases that are used in one language into their nearest equivalent in another. You have to really understand the cultural sentiments, attitudes and assumptions that lie behind the words and then find the most appropriate way of expressing them in the other language.

If, for example, a Frenchman says *C'est pas normal*, the inexperienced translator might be tempted to go for *It's not normal*. But that would be a pretty inaccurate and misleading translation. In French, the word *normal* has a cultural context. It brings to mind the whole French attitude towards logic, their Cartesian sense of the right way to think and the right way to do things. So if Jean-Claude tells you *C'est pas normal*, he expects you to be able to interpret what he means. Depending on the situation, it might be *That's completely unacceptable*; *You're approaching this in completely the wrong way*; or *He has absolutely no right to do that*.

As we saw in Chapter 1, low context communicators (such as Americans, Germans, Scandinavians, Finns) tend to express themselves in explicit, concrete, unequivocal terms. There's little cultural baggage or 'context' attached to the words they use and you can usually take what they say at face value. High context communicators (such as Arabs, Japanese, French) tend to communicate more implicitly. They expect you to be able to interpret what they mean from your knowledge of what lies behind the words, what they're actually talking about at the time, their tone of voice and, of course, their eye and body language.

English has become the lingua franca of international business. So, is it a high context or a low context language, do you think? Well, the fact is you can't always equate language with culture. When George Bernard Shaw described the British and the Americans as 'two nations divided by a common language' he wasn't just referring to the accent, or the odd difference in vocabulary. Most Americans – apart from people who come from the narrow East Coast belt – are relatively low context. Like the Germans, they will tend to say what they mean in a fairly explicit, open and direct way.

The British, on the other hand, are relatively high context – but in a rather different way from, say, the French. Our cultural conditioning has taught us that making direct and open criticisms, issuing unequivocal orders, or making *a fuss* (unnecessary demands or complaints) is very bad form. So whatever the merits or demerits of a situation, we will automatically understate them; and if we have a difficult message to deliver, we will instinctively try to soften it. We think we're being sensitive or showing a very reasonable wish to compromise. Most of the rest of world thinks we're being indecisive, pessimistic, insincere, two-faced, sarcastic... and so on. Many of our compatriots are completely unaware of the impact our communication style has on other nationalities. Your writers have known about it for a long time. And we've had a lot of practice adapting our approach to other nationalities' expectations. Even so, everything we say or write betrays our cultural conditioning – as our American readers, in particular, will have noticed from the very first page of this book.

The difference in British and American communication style doesn't just mean that the two nations *misjudge* one another. They often *misunderstand* each other too. If you're American and your British boss says: *You might like to consider changing the launch date*, what do you think he means?

A: *This is an option you should consider, but the final decision is yours.*

or

B: *I'd like you to change the launch date, please.*

Well, as you've probably guessed, he means B. Would you have realized that before you read this chapter? We know of some Americans whose boss said something similar, and they thought he meant A. So they considered changing the launch date, and decided against it. Their British boss was not impressed.

How you communicate is central to who you are and how you perceive yourself. And few people are willing – or indeed able – to behave in a way that conflicts with their own self-image. But you don't need to transform yourself into a completely different person every time you do business with someone whose values are different from yours. All you need to do is be curious, be observant, and keep an open mind. The better you understand yourself and others, the less likely you are to misinterpret your partners' motives. And the easier it will be for you to avoid sending the wrong signals to them.

Put yourself in the following situation:

> You're running an international project with very tight deadlines. Your colleague, Susan, knows that she needs to send you a detailed progress report at the end of every month. It's now 5 July and Susan's June report has only just arrived – nearly a week late. To make matters worse, some of the figures are inaccurate. You decide to call her.

How would you instinctively handle the conversation with Susan? Would you feel more comfortable taking approach A, or approach B?

Approach A

You: *I'm calling about your June report. It was a week late and some of the figures were inaccurate.*

Susan: Yes, I know. I'm sorry about that. A couple of my people were off sick.

You: *Yes but, Susan, you must respect the deadlines. If you don't, we'll fall behind schedule. And, in future, please make sure that you check all the figures very carefully.*

Approach B

You: *I'm calling about your June report.*

Susan:	I was just about to call you. I'm sorry it was late, but a couple of my people were off sick.

You:	*Oh dear... The thing is, I've just been through the figures and I'm afraid some of them don't seem to add up.*

Susan:	Don't they? Oh, I'm sorry. I had to put them together very quickly.

You:	*Right. But what about this month? Will you be able to spend a bit more time on them?*

Susan:	Yes, of course.

You:	*Great. Because, as you know, there's an important deadline coming up, and we'll be in real trouble if we miss it.*

Clearly, approach A is low context. The speaker says what he means clearly, directly and explicitly. Susan knows, without any doubt, what she has to do. Approach B, on the other hand, is high context – in a peculiarly British way. The speaker tries to avoid direct criticism or recrimination. And instead of using an imperative, he asks a question. His message is the same as speaker A's, but he tries to soften it.

Of course, we're not trying to suggest that every German, Scandinavian or American you meet would always be as frank, direct or explicit as speaker A; nor that every Brit would be as diplomatic, indirect or implicit as speaker B. What people say and the way they choose to say it depends, above all, on the relationship, what's gone before, and the actual situation. When two Brits are having a tough discussion, they're capable of using as many imperatives and concrete messages as lower context cultures do. And when the situation demands it, people from lower context cultures are equally capable of expressing themselves more indirectly or implicitly.

But, there's no denying that the way people instinctively communicate does vary from culture to culture. And unless you are aware of these differences, you may well misjudge your international colleagues' motives. If Susan were British, for example, and speaker A *always* spoke to her in this way, she could easily form the impression that he was autocratic, insensitive and uncompromising. And if she were German, American or even French, she might end up thinking that speaker B was diffident, indecisive and, possibly, insincere.

It's very hard for non-native speakers of any language – however fluent they are – to know exactly what impact they're making, or indeed to understand exactly what their native-speaking partners are saying. The high–low context communication gap compounds these problems. So if you're dealing with someone whose communication style and native tongue are different from your own, you need to think carefully about the way you're expressing yourself and to monitor the other person's reactions very closely. And if they seem confused, irritated or offended, don't just carry on; stop and ask them what's wrong. When Rosie, a colleague of ours, was giving some advice to a German client, she couldn't understand why he looked so annoyed. *You don't look very happy, Dieter*, she said. *What's the problem?* He replied: *Well, you're the trainer; I expect you to give me the answers, not ask me to supply them.* When she thought about what she had said, she realized that all her suggestions had been phrased, in typical British fashion, as questions: *Why don't you...; Wouldn't it be better if you...; How about...; What if you...* But, of course, to the low context Dieter, these turns of phrase sounded too indirect and indecisive. He expected the trainer to phrase her advice more positively and explicitly: *I think you should...; I recommend that you...; In my experience, the best way to solve this problem is...* Because she had been prepared to ask Dieter what was wrong, Rosie was soon able to clear up the misunderstanding. Dieter learnt something important about British communication style, and Rosie made sure she phrased her subsequent suggestions more positively and explicitly.

Trying to be funny

Often the British cannot be serious because they are afraid of making fools of themselves... They know and accept the rules of the game, but otherwise nothing is sacred. Nor do they draw the line at self-irony. That is why they are predestined to make compromises, the precondition for a life without absolute truths.

(Thomas Kielinger, *Crossroads and Roundabouts*, 1997)

Irony involves saying the opposite of what you mean. So it's a relatively high context way of communicating. The British love it and most people – from ambassadors to shop assistants, tycoons to taxi drivers – use it almost without thinking. Unfortunately, this style of communication doesn't always travel well:

Two British women in their early thirties were on holiday in Florida. One evening, they went to a bar where there was music and dancing. An American man, also in his thirties, politely went up to one of the women and asked her if she would like to dance. She wasn't interested in dancing, but she didn't want just to say 'No thanks' in case she offended him. So she smiled pleasantly and said: 'I won't just now, thanks. *The old war wound's playing up again*' (my war injury is causing problems). It was a line she had used, on a number of occasions, in London. British guys would usually laugh, make an equally ironic comment, and then walk away with their egos intact. But the American guy looked at her sympathetically and said: 'Hey, that's too bad. Which war were you in?' When the woman explained that she had been joking, he walked away looking confused.

Of course, there are plenty of Americans who would have seen the joke and responded with an ironic, or humorous, comment of their own. You only have to watch an episode of the popular American cartoon series, *The Simpsons*, to see that irony is alive and well in the United States. It's just that, for many Americans, irony doesn't seem to be the 'default' form of communication as it is for most Brits. As a result, Americans may sometimes take their British counterparts' ironic comments literally and, if they do, this can lead to genuine misunderstanding on both sides. So if you're British, you would be well advised to try to avoid using irony when you're doing business internationally. And if you're American, or any other nationality for whom irony is not the norm, try not to jump to the conclusion that the British are making fun of you, or being deliberately opaque. As often as not, they're making fun of themselves, or trying to defuse a tense or embarrassing situation.

Every culture has a sense of humour; everyone enjoys laughing and joking with their friends. But not everyone laughs at the same things:

A group of high potentials in a multinational company had flown to HQ from all over Europe and the United States to attend the first module of an in-house training programme. Some of the sessions were to be run by the company's own trainers; others by some of our colleagues from Canning. The first two-hour session was facilitated by one of the in-house trainers – a Norwegian. To 'break the ice', the Norwegian facilitator asked each participant to draw a self-portrait using any combination of squares, circles and triangles. The unnamed sketches were then pinned on the wall, and the Norwegian explained what the three different symbols signified. He finished with triangles, which, he solemnly told them, related to erotic characteristics. As he had hoped, the group seemed amused by this announcement and the ice was indeed broken as they tried to guess who had drawn which sketch.

The participants were then invited, one by one, to stand up and give a short self-introduction. After each presentation, the rest of the group had to try to match the speaker with one of the sketches. The last speaker was an American woman called Beth. When she told the group which sketch was hers, Steve – a British man – quietly joked to his French neighbour: 'But that can't be her. The triangles aren't big enough.' When he said 'triangles' he briefly placed his hands in front of his chest. There was a *ripple* (small wave) of laughter from the people sitting near him. The group then went to the coffee lounge for their morning break.

Shortly after the break, the Norwegian approached the Canning trainers – who were working in an adjoining room – and said: 'I need your help. The Americans are threatening to withdraw from the programme.' Our colleagues accompanied him into the seminar room and encouraged the group members to discuss what had happened. One of the Americans spoke first: 'What Steve said about Beth and the way the rest of you guys laughed constitutes sexual harassment. Back home, all of our employment contracts include a sexual harassment clause. Don't yours?' Well, no, they didn't. And it was clear that some of the Europeans found it very hard to understand their American colleagues' reaction: 'How could anyone take offence at such an innocent joke?'

Whether you sympathize with the Americans or the Europeans, the message is clear: what you think is a harmless bit of fun may well cause serious offence elsewhere. By all means show that you have a sense of humour, but stick to safe, inoffensive topics. And be aware that if you make sexist jokes in the United States, you could well end up being taken to court. Remember, too, that in a lot of places (such as Germany, Scandinavia, France, Japan), jokiness in meetings and presentations may be seen as frivolous and unprofessional. So when you're doing business with people from these cultures, keep your jokes for the bar, restaurant or sauna.

If you do join your Scandinavian colleagues for a drink, you may discover why the Norwegian facilitator was so surprised at the way Beth reacted to Steve's comment during the ice-breaker exercise:

Managers from all around the world were in Oslo to take part in a global meeting hosted by their Norwegian parent company. Our colleague Nigel was also present. On the first evening, some of the American women told him how surprised and pleased they were to see so many Norwegian women in senior positions in the company. They also commented on the number of women they had seen in the city driving taxis or working on construction sites. Back home in America's Midwest, jobs like these were normally associated with men. It was good to see that Norwegian women were so emancipated.

On the final evening, the Norwegian women gave their American sisters a demonstration of just how emancipated they were. Everyone had been invited to dinner on a Viking ship moored in Oslo harbour. There were plenty of alcoholic drinks on offer and, as the evening progressed, the jokes had become progressively more *risqué* (indecent). Suddenly, one of the Norwegian women got up and stood on her chair. With a Viking helmet on her head and a cigar in her hand, she proceeded to tell one of the most risqué jokes Nigel had ever heard. Her male and female Norwegian colleagues applauded loudly, raised their glasses and drank a special toast to her humour. The American women, on the other hand, remained silent. Nigel still remembers the look of surprise and shock on their faces.

Avoiding hidden dangers

If you passed through Heathrow airport in early 2003, you may have noticed a series of large advertising posters in which an international bank highlighted its cross-cultural expertise. The posters featured a range of gestures, colours, numbers and symbols that mean different things in different places: for example, making a circle with your thumb and forefinger which says *OK* in the United States, but something very vulgar in Mediterranean countries and the Middle East; or red, which signifies danger in much of the Western world, but symbolizes good luck to the Chinese; and so on.

Clearly, it's useful to know about differences such as these. Otherwise, you could – without realizing it – do something which causes embarrassment, distress or offence to the people you're working with. If, for example, you put four candles on a Japanese colleague's birthday cake, he may misinterpret your kind gesture: in Japan, four is a very unlucky number; it symbolizes death. If you want to get some flowers for your

French or Italian hosts, don't buy chrysanthemums; these are the flowers that people traditionally put on their family graves on All Saints Day. When you're in a meeting with someone from the Middle East, keep your feet planted firmly on the ground; showing an Arab the soles of your feet is the gravest of insults. And if you come from the Arab world, be careful about the kind of questions you ask your European colleagues:

> When I first came to London from the Middle East – at the age of 14 – I was met at the airport by a company representative whom my father had asked to look after me. As we were driving from London to Norwich, I put my foot in it: 'Who did you vote for at the last election?' I asked. 'Young man,' he replied, 'you don't ask that kind of question over here.' I found it odd and off-putting that I could not ask personal questions; that is how I had learnt to deal with people. Now I had to find another route.

And if you're American or European, avoid talking about your Arab colleagues' female relatives:

> In the Middle East you can ask questions; any questions. The only questions you do not ask are about mothers or sisters. A Saudi friend once invited an American banker to dinner at his house and introduced him to his wife. The following day, in an attempt to be polite, the banker said: 'Your wife is lovely.' He was shocked when the Arab replied: 'My wife is not the subject for conversation.'

There are a number of hidden dangers such as these. And it's worth taking the trouble to find out what they are before you start doing business in a culture that is new to you. Gestures, symbols, numbers, colours, rituals for exchanging business cards, correct seating arrangements, drinking and dining etiquette, taboo topics of conversation and so on do, of course, vary from country to country. But, unlike many of the less obvious differences that we've focused on in this chapter, they are fairly well and widely documented. You can find out what the main DOs and DON'Ts are from any reputable country guide. And we strongly recommend that you do so. After all, it would be a pity to put a promising business relationship at risk by doing something that is relatively easy to avoid.

Summary

The impulse to be courteous is universal. And most of the people you meet will be as keen to show warmth, consideration and respect as you are. But, as we've seen, you can't assume that they will do so in exactly the same way as you. No matter how carefully you do your homework, you're bound to find yourself in some situations where you simply don't know what the form is. Which is why it's so important, at all times, to keep your eyes and ears open:

- be observant;

- be curious;

- be sensitive to how others are behaving, and to the impact your behaviour seems to be having on them;

- make a conscious effort to adapt to the style and rhythm that comes naturally to the people you're dealing with;

- if they appear confused, irritated or offended, ask questions and try to clear up the misunderstanding;

- by all means show that you have a sense of humour, but stick to safe, inoffensive topics;

- above all, don't jump to hasty conclusions about what the other person is like.

5 Making presentations

You don't see something until you have the right metaphor to perceive it.

(Thomas Kuhn, *The Structure of Scientific Revolutions*, 1970)

Imagine, for a moment, that you are an area sales manager with a company that produces fast-moving consumer goods. Last quarter – January to March – the results for your region were very bad. In fact, sales were 10 per cent below target. Understandably, the sales director wants to know why there was such a serious shortfall, and how you propose to reverse the situation next quarter. He has asked you to make a presentation to him and the finance director between 10.00 and 10.30 next Monday morning.

There were a number of reasons for your area's poor performance and none of them was your fault. You have all the facts and figures to show what went wrong and why. The overriding problem, however, is that you simply don't have enough sales representatives to cover the region. You pointed this out last October when you submitted your budget, but HQ rejected your proposal to recruit extra staff.

As you sit down to prepare your presentation, which of the approaches below do you instinctively feel it would be better to take?

A   Spend most of the presentation looking back over the last quarter, making sure that your bosses understand exactly what went wrong and why.

B   Say very little about the last three months; concentrate, instead, on explaining how, with one or two extra sales representatives, you'll be able to meet, and most probably exceed, next quarter's target.

And how do you propose to give your bosses all the facts and figures you've prepared?

A Show a series of slides as you are making your presentation.

B Give them a written handout to study at their leisure afterwards.

And what about timing? How do you plan to use the 30 minutes you've got?

A Spend most of the time presenting with five minutes or so at the end for questions.

B Make a brief speech and leave at least 20 minutes for questions and discussion.

Clearly your decisions would depend, to a large extent, on how well you know the bosses, what kind of people they are, and what they're interested in. What's gone before and how much is *at stake* (to be gained or lost) would be key factors too. But if you found yourself in a similar position to this area manager, which of these approaches would come more naturally to you? And if you were one of the bosses, what would you expect from this presentation? Which of the approaches would you be more inclined to listen to?

It's quite possible that you are wondering why we're asking these questions. *It's perfectly obvious which of the approaches is right,* you may be thinking. *Why are these people insulting my intelligence?*

Well, actually, we aren't trying to insult your intelligence. The fact is, what people expect from a presentation varies from culture to culture. For example, some people think the best presentations are thorough and detailed with plenty of supporting facts and documentation; others will only listen to you if you're brief and selective. Some audiences are impressed by a logical structure; others by a creative one. Some presenters instinctively aim to inform; others to persuade or entertain. So while it may have been immediately obvious to you that approach A or B was the right one, you can't assume that your international colleagues would share your view.

But surely, you may say, *there must be some rights and wrongs that are universal; some presentation styles and techniques that are guaranteed to succeed with any audience?* Well, we wouldn't go so far as to say there are universal rights and wrongs. But there is one golden rule that successful presenters the world over follow: no matter what message they're trying to get across, they put the audience first. That may sound simple and obvious. But, as our international clients often tell us, it isn't always easy to do.

When you're having a conversation with someone, you can see or hear their reactions. And, provided you're willing to try to put yourself in their position, you can adapt what you say and the way you say it as the conversation progresses. But when you sit down to prepare a presentation, the members of your audience aren't around. You have to put the whole thing together, from start to finish, without any input or feedback from them. And you may well be tempted to concentrate on the message you want to deliver and what *you* want to achieve. As we keep repeating, however, focusing on yourself and your own agenda is the major block to successful communication, whatever context you're operating in. If you want your audience to really sit up and listen, you have to make sure that everything you say and every visual you show is interesting and relevant to them. And you can only do that if you put yourself in their *shoes* (position) at every stage.

Planning and delivering an effective presentation is hard work – even if you know your audience well and they're from the same national and corporate culture as you. When they're from a different country and you don't know them personally, it can be harder still. In our experience, the greatest challenges for an international presenter are: choosing a style that will suit the audience's expectations; putting the message you want to deliver into a concrete context that your audience can relate to; and speaking in a way that will be clear and accessible.

Choosing the right style

As we mentioned in Chapter 2, many of the management techniques that businesses adopt originate in the United States. So, too, do many of the techniques that are taught on international presentation skills courses. The Americans, perhaps more than any other culture, seem instinctively to try to build a personal rapport with their audience and to put their message across persuasively and positively. In this respect, we believe, they have a lot to teach the rest of the world. But, as our international clients often tell us, they also have a lot to learn:

When a Swiss company decided to award 'loyalty' points to their customers, they asked their in-house IT department to develop the software they needed to operate the scheme. The project was scheduled to take two years. After 18 months, however, it ran into serious difficulties. Two and a half years later, they were still trying to solve them. The company moved Connie, one of their brightest and most competent Swiss managers, on to the team. They gave her six months to get the system up and running. By June – the new deadline – she had indeed established the basic framework and solved the major difficulties. The relatively minor problems that remained could, she decided, be sorted out gradually over the next two years – at a cost of 5 million Swiss francs per year. The Swiss manager who was responsible for the loyalty scheme accepted Connie's proposal. A couple of months later, however, he left the company and was replaced by an American called Robert.

One of the first things Robert did was to ask Connie for a progress report on the project. She prepared a well-structured, informative and clear presentation. She had, in fact, performed a miracle during her six months on the team. But, being Swiss, it didn't occur to her to 'sell' herself or highlight the remarkable job she had done. Instead, she explained – in the calm, methodical, low-key style that came naturally to her – why the project had run into difficulty and what progress had been made. She then moved on to what the remaining problems were, how long it would take to solve them, and how much it would cost.

Robert was not impressed. All he heard was 'a number of problems remain' and 'it'll take two years and an additional budget of 5 million a year to solve them'. As far as he was concerned, Connie had failed to reach the targets she had been given; the problems had to be solved by the end of the current year; and he was going to put in a new team to make sure that they were. Connie didn't try to argue with him. She simply applied for a job in a different department and left the new team to take responsibility for the project. By the end of the year, they seemed to have created more problems than they had solved. The project continued for a further two years and went way over the budget Connie had projected. The Swiss were all convinced that if Robert had left Connie to handle the project her way, it would have been completed much faster and cheaper.

So why didn't Robert accept Connie's proposal? Well, we can't read his mind. But Connie, who had worked with Americans before, was convinced that it was because he had been unable to bridge the gap between American and Swiss culture. 'In my experience,' she told us,

'Robert's reaction was typically American. They always take the short-term view. They never want to hear about problems; just quick solutions. And they expect you to tell them everything is wonderful, even if it isn't. Well, I'm sorry, but that's not the way we do things in Switzerland.'

It's not the way they do things in Austria, either:

> An American manager from a large petroleum company was in Austria to meet his colleagues and visit some of the company's local petrol stations. Their Austrian manager felt there was little point in showing his American boss the outlets that were performing well. It would make more sense to show him those that were underperforming, so that he could give advice on how to solve the problems. But when the Austrian took him to the worst performing station, the American was shocked and angry: 'Why did you bring me here? I don't want to see this. Take me to a station that's doing well.'

While the Americans would be likely to lean towards the left of the following scales, the Swiss and Austrians would probably lean towards the right.

Short-term						Long-term				
I prefer to focus on the here and now.						I need to see beyond the horizon and plan accordingly.				
50	40	30	20	10	0	10	20	30	40	50
Upbeat						Low-key				
I always try to emphasize the positive aspects of a situation. And I'm not afraid to talk openly about my own achievements and successes.						I always try to give a factual and balanced view of a situation. And if I've done a good job, I let the facts speak for themselves.				
50	40	30	20	10	0	10	20	30	40	50

As everyone knows, of course, the United States is a relatively young country. It was only in 1620 that the Pilgrim Fathers settled in Plymouth, Massachusetts – the first permanent colony in New England. There have been many waves of other immigrants since then, most of them trying to escape the religious persecution, political unrest or extreme poverty of the old world; and all of them attracted by the freedom and opportunities that were on offer. Between the 1840s and the early 1920s, for example, some 30 million people immigrated to the United States. These immigrants were determined to build a new and better life for themselves. They were convinced that, with hard work and a little luck, there would be no limit to what they could achieve. Naturally enough, their attitudes and expectations have had a strong influence on American cultural values.

According to *The Stuff Americans are Made Of* (Hammond and Morrison, 1996), there are seven cultural forces that define Americans:

- they insist on choice;

- they pursue *impossible* dreams;

- they are obsessed with *big* and *more*;

- they are impatient with time;

- they accept mistakes;

- they have an urge to improvise;

- they have a fixation with what is new.

These seven forces, say Hammond and Morrison, link together like this:

> Our freedom of *choice* allows us to tackle an *'impossible'* dream that is *bigger* than anything we've done before; we want to achieve it *now*; but *fail* in our initial attempts; we try again and through some sort of improvisation succeed, only to wonder *what's new* so that we can start all over and make another *choice*.

It's hardly surprising, then, that Robert was unimpressed by Connie's *low-key* presentation, rejected her *two-year* schedule, and decided to put a *new* team in. But, as we've seen, this was the wrong decision. There are plenty of people in the world – from countries as diverse as Japan, Switzerland and the United Kingdom – whose culture has taught them to take a longer-term view; who instinctively express themselves in a low-key way; and who would be embarrassed to talk openly about their own achievements. That doesn't mean they're incompetent, pessimistic or lacking in dynamism.

But Connie was the presenter, you may say. *So surely it was up to her to adapt her style to suit Robert's expectations*. Well, yes, you're quite right.

She should have tried to sound more positive and even, perhaps, to emphasize the remarkable progress that had been made during the first half of the year. But, she was a Swiss woman, working at the Swiss head-quarters of a Swiss company. She knew, of course, that Robert spoke no German. And she was perfectly happy to make her presentation in English. But it didn't occur to her that she needed to adapt her style too. In any case, she knew she had done a first-rate job; and she knew her Swiss bosses valued her highly. As far as her career and reputation were concerned, Robert's opinion was irrelevant.

For most presenters, though, choosing the right style to suit their audience is vital:

> George, a senior fund manager with a British asset management firm (let's call them BAM) came to Canning to polish up a presentation he was going to make to his firm's largest American client. His aim was to persuade the Americans to renew BAM's mandate. The trouble was, the performance figures for the previous and current year looked very bad, and the Americans were threatening to take their business elsewhere. George would have just half an hour to change their minds. He was planning to spend most of that time looking back over the previous 18 months, and justifying the way in which BAM had managed the fund. His trainer Richard persuaded him to take a much more upbeat approach. Instead of looking at what had gone wrong in the past, George tried to focus on the good results BAM could achieve in future: 'Stay with BAM and we'll beat the target you have set us' was his new central message. This new approach made his presentation much shorter. George practised it again and again, paying particular attention to his tone of voice. By the end of the two-day coaching session, he knew the introduction and conclusion off by heart. And he really *sounded* positive and optimistic.
>
> The following week, George phoned Richard in triumph: 'They've renewed the mandate', he said. 'Thank God you made me change my central message! When I arrived, their consultant told me I had only 5 minutes, not 30. So I just went in and presented the introduction and conclusion. According to their consultant, the trustees were very impressed that I had been able to adapt so flexibly to the time constraint. And they had confidence in me because I sounded so positive and didn't give them any of the "usual British bullshit".'
>
> On the strength of this five-minute presentation, over a hundred million dollars of pension fund money were allocated.

All of us carry around very fixed images of other cultures. These stereo-types are often negative, and nearly always the result of measuring what foreigners do or say against our own cultural norms. When George's client referred to the *usual British bullshit*, we knew exactly what he meant. On our cross-cultural workshops, we always ask the participants how they perceive other nationalities. And we have discovered that the image the Americans and British have of one another is remarkably consistent. For example, on one course we ran for the European head office of a major American company, the expatriate American managers said that, in their view, the British were:

▨ always talking about problems, not solutions;

▨ always focusing on what has happened, and not on what will happen;

▨ *gloomy* (pessimistic) and depressing, even when they are giving good news;

▨ rude and disrespectful;

▨ badly prepared.

The trouble is, taking the kind of upbeat, positive attitude that impresses the Americans doesn't come naturally to the British. As we saw in Chapter 4, our culture values understatement, irony and self-deprecation. Maybe that's why the British managers on the course told us that, in their view, the Americans were:

▨ always over-optimistic;

▨ not prepared to analyse a problem properly in order to reach workable solutions;

▨ boastful and superficial;

▨ not prepared to disagree with superiors, even when they are wrong;

▨ badly prepared.

Some years ago, Canning was considering the possibility of offering an e-learning service. We invited a number of software consultancies to present their proposals for a tailored solution. One of the consultancies was American and they flew two of their vice-presidents over to the United Kingdom to do some research and make their proposal. The presenters were friendly, dynamic and enthusiastic. They started their presentation something like this: *It's a real privilege for us to be here. And we're very excited about the prospect of handling this project for you.* They then spent what seemed like 20 minutes telling us, in glowing terms, about their personal experience and many successes. As they spoke, they showed us slide after slide, and animated graphic after animated graphic, taken from the e-learning programmes they had developed for other clients – few of whom seemed to be in the same business as Canning. When they finally started talking about us, it was immediately clear that they had little understanding of our training style or our clients' needs. During the question and answer session at the end, we raised many objections to their proposals. Instead of trying to answer these objections, they simply said things like: *We've got a lot of experience in this field. We'll be able to work through that kind of issue when the project's under way.*

The audience were all international communication trainers who were more prepared than most to make an effort to bridge the culture gap. And if these presenters had been able to show us that they really understood our business, we would have forgiven them for the emphasis they had placed on their own achievements and successes. But because they weren't prepared to engage with the problems we raised, we left the presentation feeling mildly angry that they had wasted so much of our time. And even we allowed ourselves to think, for a few moments, that their performance had been *typically American*. In other words, that it had conformed to most of the negative images in the list above.

Clearly, when you're presenting internationally, you have to make a conscious effort to avoid reinforcing negative stereotypes such as these. If not, there's a danger you will alienate the audience almost as soon as you open your mouth. That's not to say you should try to change your natural style so radically that you feel uncomfortable. No one could have expected the American software consultants to stop sounding enthusiastic and positive. Indeed, we believe that putting your message across persuasively and positively is something that all presenters should aim to do. But there has to be something behind the positive noises you're making. You've got to show the audience that you understand their needs and expectations. And you've got to make sure that everything you say is relevant and interesting to them. The American consultants seemed to have made little effort to understand us. And the many successes and achievements that they presented were simply not relevant. That was why we found them superficial and boastful. If they had put us first, we would probably have been very favourably impressed by their upbeat and dynamic style.

Similarly, when Canning was helping George from BAM to prepare his presentation, we did not, for one moment, expect him to say anything that made him feel uncomfortable. We didn't, for example, ask him to tell his clients how excited he was about the prospect of managing the fund next year. We simply suggested that, to suit the expectations of his American audience, he should try to look forward rather than back. And once he did that, he was able to find a central message, *Stay with BAM and we'll beat the target you have set us*, that his clients could relate to. His whole presentation was structured around this upbeat, forward-looking message. So when he only had time to deliver the introduction and conclusion, it came across loud and clear to his clients. All the more so because he tried very hard to *sound* positive and optimistic.

It would be wrong to assume, from the examples we've looked at, that the British and Americans are at opposite ends of every scale. The two cultures actually have a lot of views and values in common. Both nations would, for example, probably fall to the left of the following scales:

Short						**Long**				
I keep my presentation short and to the point, never go over an agreed time limit, and speak as concisely as possible.						I allocate as much time to the subject as it deserves and try to speak as eloquently and impressively as possible.				
50	40	30	20	10	0	10	20	30	40	50
Selective						**Comprehensive**				
I select only the key points and avoid clouding my message with unnecessary detail.						I make sure my presentation is thorough and detailed with plenty of supporting facts and documentation.				
50	40	30	20	10	0	10	20	30	40	50

Of course, there are plenty of American and British presenters who include a lot of detail and talk at considerable length. The American software consultants spent 20 minutes telling us about their successes and achievements; and George originally planned to talk to his clients for half an hour. But the American presentation didn't succeed; and George's original structure and style would have lost him the mandate. In general, American and British audiences respond best to presentations that are short and selective. As you might expect, not every culture shares their expectations:

> An English manager was at a meeting in Milan. The Italian partici-
> pants belonged to a network of professional service companies who
> wanted to pool their skills. Each of the delegates had been asked to
> prepare a *brief* presentation of their company. The Englishman was
> annoyed to find that his fellow delegates ignored the request to
> keep their presentations *brief* and in some cases spoke for as long
> as 20 minutes. When it was his turn to speak, he delivered a two-
> minute presentation. It had a clear message, was well structured
> and gave the key information relevant to his listeners. As he sat
> down, there was an awkward silence; and then polite applause.
> After the meeting, which finished two hours late, an Italian friend
> came up to the Englishman. 'Why', he asked, 'didn't you explain in
> much greater detail the many things I know your company can offer
> the group?'

Where you would place yourself on the short–long and selective–compre-
hensive scales will be heavily influenced by the educational norms in your country. At school and university in Italy, the examinations are often oral. So, throughout their education, Italian students are taught all the rhetor-
ical skills; and they learn to give long, impressive speeches that will show their examiners how much they have learnt and thought about the subject. Naturally enough, when they come to make a business presentation, they take the same approach. They aim to be eloquent and positive; and, of course, to speak for as long as it takes to show the audience that they have thought of all the points.

The British education system, on the other hand, encourages a crisper, more concise style. When your writers were at school, we had lessons and exams where we had to précis texts – in other words, reduce several pages of complicated prose into one short, simple paragraph. As we mentioned above, we were also conditioned, from a very early age, to understate our abilities and give our messages indirectly. When the Englishman made his short, low-key presentation, he was really sending the signal 'less is more'. This would have been fine for a British audience, but the message was completely *lost on* (misunderstood by) his Italian listeners. The structure he chose came across to them as over-simplistic and far too low-key. They expected him to illustrate the facts with relevant examples and opinions, to argue his case with eloquence, and to project a positive and upbeat attitude.

To most Brits, the word *rhetoric* describes a speech that sounds impressive, but isn't actually sincere or useful. For the Italians, however, it's the art of speaking eloquently, impressively and persuasively. *Rhetorik* is also an important part of the academic and business school syllabus in Germany. But the Germans seem to interpret the word in a different way again. In his comparative study of German and British culture (*Crossroads and Roundabouts*, 1997), Thomas Kielinger suggests that his fellow Germans most value people who are *konsequent* (logical, consistent, uncompromising) and *grundlich* (thorough). So, for them, *Rhetorik* is the art of presenting a logical and detailed sequence of arguments – as reflected in the dialectical methods of Hegel and Marx. For German students to pass their oral exams, there's no need for them to put forward a lot of new or original ideas. They simply have to learn all the facts and present them in a logical and thorough way.

Maybe that's why the Germans tend to dislike presentations that sound like a sales pitch. While the Italians, Americans and Brits would fall to the left of the scale below, the Germans would most probably fall to the right:

Persuade						Inform				
I state my own opinions and conclusions upfront and focus only on those areas that support my argument.						I give a detailed and balanced view of the whole situation, so that the audience can draw their own conclusions.				
50	40	30	20	10	0	10	20	30	40	50

So, if you're presenting to a German audience, avoid the hard sell. Try, instead, to construct a logical and convincing argument using plenty of relevant facts. And if you're German, remember that – with the possible exception of the Scandinavians, Finns and Japanese – few other cultures are as fascinated by exhaustive lists of facts as you are. So make a conscious effort to select only the data that support your central message and are relevant and interesting to your audience. If you don't, there's a very real danger that they will fall asleep. That doesn't mean you should abandon your logical approach – particularly if you're presenting to the French. The French, like the Germans, would fall at the far right of this scale:

Creative structure						Logical structure				
What I appreciate most is a creative structure that surprises and intrigues.						What I appreciate most is a well-structured, logical sequence of arguments.				
50	40	30	20	10	0	10	20	30	40	50

The French enjoy debate, value eloquence and, above all, expect the presenter to give them a logically consistent argument that can't be demolished. In French schools, pupils are taught to present their arguments in a very Cartesian way: *thèse, anti-thèse, synthèse* (thesis, antithesis, synthesis). As we mentioned earlier, many of the techniques that are taught on international presentation skills courses originate in the United States. And the Americans tend to state their central message at the beginning of their presentation. But this technique does not come naturally to the French. That's because a good central message is effectively a synthesis or conclusion. And the French are taught from an early age to lead up to the conclusion step by step – not state it upfront at the beginning.

It's quite possible that, at this point, your head is starting to spin. Don't worry! There may be over 200 countries in the world, but we aren't going to try to talk about all of them. The cultures we have looked at, and the scales we have shown you, cover the main style differences you will come across. Before you can adapt to your audience's expectations, you need to do two things: first, analyse your own style and preferences as objectively as possible; and second, resist the temptation to believe that you are right and the rest of the world is wrong. If you know yourself, keep an open mind and make every effort to know your audience, you can always find a way to bridge even the widest culture gap.

Finding a concrete context

In a typical year, many of the international business people we work with have to attend at least 25 presentations. But when we ask them how many of these presentations they would describe as really impressive or memorable, their answer is nearly always the same: *No more than 20 per cent.* So what do the presenters who belong to this elite minority do that sets them apart from everyone else? Well, part of the answer is in the quotation at the head of this chapter: they realize that people only see something when they have the right metaphor to perceive it.

Imagine for a moment that you work for a large pharmaceutical company which is about to launch an anti-fungal cream. As product manager, it's your job to present the new cream and ways of selling it to each of the four regional sales teams in your country. So what do you think you should do: deliver exactly the same presentation to each of the four teams; or try to adapt it each time?

In our experience, most people would see nothing wrong with delivering exactly the same presentation to each of the teams. And many would also assume that, in this situation, it would be perfectly acceptable to let the facts speak for themselves. *After all,* they argue, *there's no need to agonize over what might appeal to these audiences. They all work for the same company and they're all salespeople. So they're bound to be interested in the product and how to sell it.*

Well, yes, that may be true. But it doesn't mean they will necessarily be fascinated by what you have to say. What if they already know a lot of the information you're planning to present? What if they've already decided that some of your new sales policies are wrong or unsuitable for their region? What if the members of one team are at war with their colleagues in one of the other teams?

It doesn't matter how relevant you think the subject matter is, you've still got to try to put it in a context that the audience can relate to. And, as every audience is different, you're going to have to change the context to suit each one. We don't believe you can create a universal presentation that will be equally relevant and memorable to a series of different listeners. What interests and appeals to one group may well bore or irritate another.

The situation we asked you to imagine – like all the situations in this book – was a real one. After some research and careful thought, the product manager concerned came up with a neat way of making his message relevant to each of the teams. He had discovered that nearly all the sales representatives were keen football fans. So he worked out a way of describing the new sales strategy in footballing terms: the sales team was to be divided into strikers who would go out and find new customers, defenders who would concentrate on cultivating existing customers, sweepers who would be sent out to solve problems, and so on. He was sure that this metaphor would be equally attractive to each of the four sales teams. But he knew it would have even greater impact if he could show them a picture.

That was when he realized how he could tailor his presentation to each region. He got his graphics department to prepare four different visuals. Each one showed football players wearing the colours of the top local team. When he showed the visual, the sales reps immediately identified with the players and started teasing one another. On a couple of occasions, their jokes gave the product manager a clearer understanding of their needs. And he was able to adapt his presentation accordingly.

But what can I do, our clients often ask us, *if I don't know the people I'm presenting to?* Well, if you don't know the members of your audience personally, ask yourself what you know about them as a group: are they, for example, all engineers; do they all come from India; are they all in their twenties? You have to keep asking questions about them until you find some common denominator.

But what if the audience do different jobs, come from different countries, and are different ages? you may ask. Surely the only common denominator then is the information I'm going to present. Well, no. You're forgetting the most important thing they have in common. They're all human beings. And no matter where they come from or what they do, all human beings have certain needs and aims in common. It's just a question of finding which of their needs and aims you could most effectively appeal to in this particular presentation. Often, the answers won't come to you straight away. But if you want your audience to really take notice of what you're saying, you need to persevere.

Finding a context and developing a concrete image your audience can relate to takes time, patience, effort, and a bit of imagination. But it isn't rocket science. In fact, as the example below shows, it's often the simplest ideas that work best:

Our colleague Richard was running a presentations course for a group of six Finns. They worked for a large industrial conglomerate whose core business was paper production. On the first day, Richard invited each of them to make a short presentation about their company. The first five presentations were almost identical: 'Our company employs thousands of people in many different countries. We have factories in this town, that town and the other town. We produce paper, paper-making machinery, drilling platforms, power plants...' and so on, and so on, and so on. Richard was desperate for a cup of coffee. Even so, he decided to get the last presentation out of the way before the mid-morning break. The sixth guy was called Matti and his presentation went something like this:

Matti: Richard.

Richard: (surprised) Yes?

Matti: Which newspaper do you read?

> Richard: (even more surprised) *The Guardian.*
>
> Matti: *Ah! That's a paper for students and left-wingers, right?*
>
> Richard: (impressed) Well, I suppose it is, yeah. I started reading it when I was a student. Though I'm more of a liberal democrat these days.
>
> Matti: *OK. But what problems do you have when you read* The Guardian?
>
> Richard: Well, I don't always agree with their politics. And they make a lot of spelling mistakes.
>
> Matti: *And what about your hands? What do they look like when you have finished reading the paper?*
>
> Richard: My hands? Well, pretty dirty usually. It's a real nuisance.
>
> Matti: *Exactly. And you're one of our customers, Richard. We supply over 30 per cent of the newsprint that's used in the United Kingdom. And we want you to have clean hands. That's why our R&D people are trying to find a way of keeping the ink on the paper and off your hands. You see...*
>
> Richard was hooked. He forgot all about the coffee break and would have been happy to let Matti speak for far longer than the three minutes he had been allotted.

Matti ended up presenting more or less the same information as his five colleagues. But unlike them, he put Richard first. He focused on the human element and found a concrete example that Richard could immediately relate to. As a result, Richard really listened to him and, to this day, still remembers what he said.

Clearly, Richard and Matti have quite a lot in common. They're both Europeans; they're both from developed, stable democracies; they're both widely travelled. So it was relatively easy for Matti to put himself in Richard's shoes. Finding the right context for an audience whose cultural values and expectations are very different from yours can be more challenging. That's because many of your perceptions are so instinctive you don't ever consider whether there might be another way of looking at the world. This was certainly the case for Al – a young American Peace Corps volunteer – whom Richard worked with in Africa in the 1970s:

Al was in his early twenties when he arrived at the junior high school in a large village in southern Africa to teach mathematics. The village consisted of traditional mud huts where the 40,000 inhabitants lived, the school (eight large rectangular buildings), a church and a hospital (both built by Scottish missionaries). At first, Al was very impressed with the pupils' enthusiasm and aptitude for his subject. But when he moved on to geometry – starting with squares, rectangles and triangles, as he did in the States – they seemed to lose interest. They simply couldn't see the point of the exercises their teacher was asking them to do. After a particularly frustrating lesson, Al went for a walk to clear his head. He climbed a nearby hill, stood at the top, and looked down at the village. 'But of course!', he thought. 'Most of the buildings in the village are circular. No wonder they're not interested in right angles. Why didn't I see that before?'

Next day, he started the maths class by saying: 'I want you to imagine you're an eagle. You're looking down on the village. What do you see?' The children immediately drew a lot of circular huts and walls. 'OK', said the teacher. 'So how much space do you have in each hut? And how far is it from the edge of the hut to the edge of the wall?' From that moment on, the children were hooked. They eagerly learned about 'pi', and were soon working out circumferences and areas. And they were just as interested when the teacher moved from circles to tangents and from tangents to angles.

From a Western perspective, it makes no sense to start with circles and end with squares. In fact, that's doing things *the wrong way round*. But for these young Africans, it was *the right way round*. And the American teacher only realized that when he started to see the world through his pupils' eyes. Making a conscious effort to step outside your own cultural preconceptions is the key to finding the right context for your international audiences.

Sooner or later, you will make or attend a presentation where one of the visuals is a map. When you learnt geography at school, you probably assumed that the maps your teachers gave you were universal. After all, everyone lives in the same world and countries are a fixed shape and size. And it probably never occurred to you that different cultures see the world, literally, through different eyes:

A Swedish professor was presenting the results of some clinical trials at an international pharmaceutical symposium in Florence. A high proportion of the delegates were from the Middle East and Asia. To show where the people who had taken part in the trial came from, the professor had a slide with a map of the world on it. Instead of illustrating his point, however, the slide seemed to be confusing the audience. Some of them frowned, others exchanged glances, and one or two of them raised their eyebrows. From that point on, the professor sensed that he had lost the audience's attention. 'I can't understand what the problem was', he confided to a friend several days later. 'I mean, this is the slide I used. Can you see anything wrong with it?' His friend looked at the slide for a moment, smiled and asked: 'Where did you get this map from?' The professor replied: 'I don't know. The people in our graphics department produced all the slides. Why?' His friend said: 'Well, they shouldn't have put Sweden right at the centre of the map, should they?' The professor looked puzzled: 'But that's where most of the clinical trials took place.' His friend shook his head and pointed to the tiny landmass that represented the Indian sub-continent: 'Yes, but most of your audience came from this part of the world. I expect they were pretty shocked to see that you thought Sweden was three times the size of India.'

The world map that many Americans and Europeans are used to seeing is based on Mercator's projection. And according to Mercator's projection, North America is bigger than Africa, Scandinavia is bigger than India, and Europe is bigger than South America. But, in fact, this is a gross distortion of the world. A map using an equal area projection (eg Arno Peters') reveals that North America is far smaller than Africa; India is three times the size of Scandinavia; and South America is twice the size of Europe. When we show a Peters' world map on our presentation courses, some of the participants react quite negatively. They declare that it's *wrong*; that the continents are *shaped wrongly*. Maybe they expect the industrialized countries to look bigger than the developing ones because they're richer. Or maybe they've simply never realized that the world maps they've always used give an inaccurate impression of each country's size and are, therefore, not universally accepted.

That was certainly the case with the Swedish professor. The last thing he wanted to do was offend or alienate his audience. If only he had asked someone from India or the Middle East for their advice while he was preparing his presentation. It's such a simple and obvious thing to do. And yet, in our experience, it's something that far too many presenters forget – particularly when the presentation they're preparing involves a lot of creative work:

A large European company were trying to sell their high-tech systems to clients around the world. They tailored each presentation to the individual client's interests, but there was one key metaphor and visual that they always used: 'Your problems', they told their clients, 'are like lions – wild, unpredictable, and hard to control. But with our systems, you can be a lion tamer. You can subdue the lions and keep them under control.' This worked very well until they went to a country in Africa. As soon as they showed the visual, the audience looked horrified. The lion was a symbol of their country, and the image that came across to them was of a colonial power subduing their state. The Europeans lost the contract to a competitor.

The trouble was, these Europeans had invested a lot of time, money and effort in developing the lion-tamer image. In any case, it had already been tried out on a number of audiences and worked very well. So they didn't see any reason why it shouldn't succeed with their prospective African clients too. For the international presenter, this is a dangerous position to be in. It's only human nature to believe that an idea you've worked hard to create is sure to succeed. But before you get too attached to it, you need to check it out with a local expert, and act on the advice they give you. And you should never assume that, just because an image has already succeeded with one audience, it will necessarily have the right impression on another. Remember, every audience is different. What engages and amuses one group of people may mystify or offend another.

Speaking with impact

There's one thing, however, that every audience in the world has in common. If a presenter uses language that is unclear, or speaks in an over-complicated or monotonous way, they will fall asleep.

Try reading the sentence below out loud:

With the installation of our new manufacturing software platform and the implementation of the seven-step quality initiative, which, as some of you are probably aware, represent a substantial investment of some 15 million, our ultimate objective, once these two projects have been implemented at the end of next year, is the achievement of optimal production performance, a reduction in lead times, and an overall improvement to customer service...

It sounds horrible, doesn't it? If you speak like this, you'll lose your audience's attention before you even get to the end of your first sentence. So what's going wrong here? Well, more or less everything, to be honest.

For a start, there are far too many nouns: *installation, implementation, investment, objective, achievement, performance, reduction, improvement.* And look at them. They're all very long – three syllables or more; and most of them are very abstract. Can you actually visualize *implementation, achievement* or *performance?* You certainly couldn't draw a picture to explain what these abstractions mean. And listen to the rhythm: instalLATion, implemenTATion, inVESTment, and so on. In every case, the stress falls on the next to last syllable. That kind of rhythm is guaranteed to send an audience to sleep – as your writers know from long experience of listening to the first presentations our clients make when they come on one of our courses.

So why do people use these long abstract nouns? Well, for the native speaker of English, they're the kind of words you find in very formal, written documents – economic reports, academic theses and contracts, for example. So they probably think that using them in their presentation will make them sound more intellectual or impressive. And, of course, a lot of non-native speakers use these words all the time – particularly the Germans and the Italians – because that's the way they speak in their own language.

But English is a language that loves verbs. If you want your audience to be able to visualize what you're saying, you need to talk about people doing things. For example:

We're going to *install* some new production software.

We're going to *set up* a better quality control system.

We're *investing* more than 15 million in these projects.

What we're *aiming* to do is *boost* output, *cut* lead times, and *improve* customer satisfaction.

All these verbs are short – no more than two syllables. And the minute you start using them, you can help your audience understand what you're saying by stressing the parts of the sentence that you think are important. For example:

We're going to install some NEW production SOFTware and SET UP a BETter quality conTROL system.

You see, in natural spoken English, every sentence is a combination of long beats and short beats, rather like the drum rhythm in a pop song. As soon as you stress the important parts of the sentence, you adopt this natural rhythm. And you start sounding like a real person talking to other real people – rather than someone who is reading from a script, or delivering a pedantic lecture.

So the sentence we asked you to read out loud has far too many long, abstract nouns. But that's not the only thing that's wrong with it. The sentence itself is much too long. Successful international presenters keep their sentences short and simple. If you try to put too many ideas into one sentence, you'll be forced to use subordinate clauses: *which, as some of you are probably aware, represent a substantial investment of some 15 million*; and *once these two projects have been implemented at the end of next year*. And subordinate clauses make it very difficult for your listeners to remember how the sentence began. If you want to speak with impact, aim for one idea per sentence. And, where possible, keep your sentences active:

instead of:	*once these two projects <u>have been implemented</u>* (passive verb construction)
say:	*once <u>we've implemented</u> these two projects* (active verb construction)
instead of:	*The new machines <u>were checked</u> by us.*
say:	*<u>We checked</u> the new machines.*

Of course, there will be occasions when you need to use a passive construction. You may well prefer, for example, to say *a lot of mistakes were made* rather than *the sales director made a lot of mistakes*. But when you're not worried about saying who did what, active sentences generally have far greater impact.

So if you follow all the advice above, and also try to add some 'you-appeal' – in other words, make sure that what you're saying is relevant to the audience – this speech might sound something like this:

What can we do to boost our output? How can we cut lead times? How can we improve customer service? These are questions you've been asking for some time. And today, I've got some answers for you. We've decided to spend 15 million updating our systems. First, we're going to install the latest production software. And, second, we're going to set up a much tighter quality control system. Both projects should be up and running by the end of next year...

OK. Are you ready for a short exercise? If so, look at the sentence below, and work out how you would replace the nouns with verbs:

It is necessary to have a detailed examination of the specification before the installation of the new line.

If you are a non-native speaker of English, you will probably instinctively say something like this:

We *need* to *examine* the specification very carefully before we *install* the new line.

If you are a native English speaker, your proposal may be more like this:

We *need* to *go through* the spec with a fine-tooth comb before we *put* the new line *in*.

English has an enormous vocabulary – twice as big, for example, as French. Words are derived from two main language streams: Germanic (German and Scandinavian) and Romance (Latin-based). As you will see in Chapter 7, native speakers tend automatically to choose short Germanic verbs (for example: *get, go through, put in, tell*) in preference to their Latin-based equivalents (*obtain, examine, install, inform*). That's because, to their ear, Latin-based verbs sound too formal for speaking, and are more appropriate for writing – rather like the long, abstract nouns we looked at above.

But non-native speakers have most probably learnt *written* rather than *spoken* English. This means that they are likely to feel far more comfortable with words that are derived from Latin. Even people, like the Japanese, whose own language has no connection with Latin, tend to feel this way. And, somewhat paradoxically, many Germans prefer Latin-based words too. That's because they sound more formal and, therefore, more similar to High German. We still have Germans on our language courses who believe that *get* isn't correct English. And, of course, to speakers of Romance languages – French, Spanish, Italian, Portuguese, Romanian – Latin-based words are much easier to understand.

The fact that English has become the common language of international business should be very good news for the monolingual American, Australian, New Zealander or Brit. All too often, however, the native English speaker is at a disadvantage. Some years ago, an East Asian airline chose to buy flight simulators from a French firm rather than a British one: as their pilots would have to be trained in English to use the simulators, the airline preferred to buy them from the people who spoke the clearer English – in other words, the French. And one of Italy's top companies refuses to have American or British consultants running their courses; they prefer Swiss or Dutch people who can speak English in a way that will be understood by all their staff.

If you're a native English speaker and you're presenting to an audience for whom English is a second or foreign language, you need to choose the kind of verbs they're likely to understand. That means, for example, saying *examine* rather than *go through*; and *install* instead of *put in*. And rather than use idiomatic expressions like *with a fine-tooth comb* and abbreviations like *spec*, you should say *very carefully* and *specification* instead.

And try to control your tone and tempo. Many presenters, particularly native speakers, make the mistake of speaking too *fast*. But, of course, if you speak too *slowly*, you could sound artificial and patronizing. The secret is to keep your natural tone, enunciate clearly, and pause at the end of a phrase or sentence – *not* after each word. When you're rehearsing your presentation, record part of your speech and listen to yourself critically. Do you sound natural? Are the pauses long enough? Whoever you're presenting to, you'll need to pause more frequently and for longer than you do in normal conversation.

Even if you're a native speaker presenting to a native-speaking audience, you can't assume that they will immediately understand what your main points are and how they link together. Listening to a presentation isn't like reading a book. Your audience can't *see* when you are 'starting a new paragraph'. If they miss a step in your argument, they can't go back and 'read' it again. It's your job, as presenter, to guide your audience through your speech. At every step, you need to tell them where they are, where they've been, and where they're going. So try to create plenty of beginnings, where you summarize your argument so far, and tell them what the next step is.

Summary

Wherever your audience is from, your presentation will only be successful if they really listen to what you're saying and remember the message you're trying to get across. Following the guidelines below will help you achieve this objective.

Know your audience

▨ Who are they?

▨ How much do they already know about the subject?

▨ How do they feel about it – hostile, neutral or positive?

▨ What will they gain from listening to you?

▨ What are they expecting?

Create a central message

Try to express in one clear, punchy sentence what the presentation is about and what the audience will gain from listening to you. In his introduction, for example, George told his American clients: *I'm going to show you how, if you stay with BAM, we will beat the target you have set us.* This has much more 'you-appeal' than his original central message: *A lot of things went wrong last quarter but, as you will see, this was out of our control.*

Choose the right style

Even if you're presenting to an audience who value a lot of facts and background information, it's still vital to be selective. The most dangerous subject for you as presenter is the one that fascinates you; the one that you're the world expert on. If you're in this position, check your motives. Why are you including this point? Is it because your audience really needs to know it? Or is it just because you find it interesting – and, perhaps, want to show people how much you know?

Choose only the points that support your central message and are relevant to your audience. Ask yourself at which end of the selective – comprehensive and short – long scales your audience falls. If they are, for example, German, Scandinavian or Japanese, support what you say with plenty of relevant facts and figures. If, on the other hand, they're from the United States or the United Kingdom, go for a broad overview which includes only details that are absolutely essential.

If you're presenting to the Americans, focus on future solutions rather than past problems and don't be afraid to give your own opinions and recommendations upfront. If your audience is from Germany, on the other hand, avoid the hard sell. Try, instead, to give a detailed, balanced and logical view of the advantages and disadvantages. And if your audience is French, make sure that your argument is logical and consistent.

Find a concrete context

Even if the members of your audience seem to have nothing in common with each other, keep asking yourself questions until you find a common denominator. Remember, people only see something when they have the right metaphor to perceive it. Finding that metaphor will often turn a satisfactory presentation into a brilliant one.

Speak with impact

▦ Keep your sentences short, simple and active.

▦ Avoid long abstract nouns.

▦ Use the verbs your audience will understand.

▦ Avoid expressions like *with a fine-tooth comb* and abbreviations like *spec*.

▦ Stress the important parts of the sentence.

▦ Pause after each phrase and sentence.

▦ At every step, tell the audience where they are, where they've been, and where they're going.

6 Making deals

*Let us never negotiate out of fear. But let us never fear to
negotiate. Let both sides explore what problems unite us
instead of belaboring those problems which divide us...
Together let us explore the stars...*

(John F Kennedy – Inaugural address, 20 January 1961)

Have you noticed that when a deal *falls through* (fails), most negotiators automatically blame some practical issue: *the client couldn't afford to pay for the kind of quality we offer*; or *we don't have the capacity to supply the volumes they're looking for.* Very few people are prepared to admit that they lost the contract because they didn't handle the client or the negotiation in the right way.

In the international arena, however, it's your negotiating style above all else that can make or break a deal:

Two companies had been short-listed for a major infrastructural contract in Mexico. One was from the United States, the other Swedish. Both companies were invited to Mexico to present their proposals to the relevant ministry and to start negotiating the terms of a deal.

The Americans put a lot of effort into producing a high-tech, hard-hitting presentation. Their message was clear: 'We can give you the most technically advanced equipment at a price our competitors can't match.' The team – which consisted of senior technical experts, lawyers and interpreters – flew down from their New York head office to Mexico City, where they had reserved rooms in one of the top hotels for a week. In order to put on the best possible performance for the minister and his officials, the Americans had arranged to give their presentation in a conference room at the hotel; and they had brought all the necessary equipment with them from the States. All the arrangements had been written down in great detail and sent to the Mexican officials two weeks earlier.

At the agreed time the American team were ready to present, but they had no one to present to. The people from the ministry arrived at various times over the next hour. They didn't apologize for being late, but just began to chat amiably with the Americans about a wide range of non-business matters. The leader of the American team kept glancing anxiously at his watch. Finally, he suggested that the presentation should start. Though the Mexicans seemed surprised, they politely agreed, and took their seats. Twenty minutes later the minister – accompanied by some senior officials – walked in. He looked extremely angry and asked the Americans to start the presentation again from the beginning. Ten minutes later, he started talking to an aide who had just arrived with a message for him. When the American presenter stopped speaking, the minister signalled that he should continue. By this time, most of the audience were talking amongst themselves. When invited to ask questions at the end, the only thing the minister wanted to know was why the Americans had told them so little about their company's history.

Later, during lunch, the Americans were very surprised to be asked questions about their individual backgrounds and qualifications, rather than the technical details of their products. The Minister had a brief word with the American team leader and left without eating or drinking anything.

Over the next few days, the Americans contacted their Mexican counterparts several times in an attempt to fix a meeting and start the negotiations. They reminded them that they had to fly back to the States at the end of the week. But the Mexicans' response was always the same: 'We need time to examine your proposal amongst ourselves first.' At the end of the week the Americans left Mexico angry, frustrated and empty-handed.

It was the Swedes who won this lucrative contract, and we'll have a look at how they handled the initial stages of the negotiation later. But first, let's try to work out why, despite their best intentions, things went so badly wrong for these negotiators from the United States. There's no doubt that they really wanted this contract. And they clearly invested a lot of time, money and effort in trying to make the best possible impression:

they picked a first rate team; they looked round for a prestigious venue; they scheduled a carefully timed itinerary; they planned a comprehensive agenda; they put together an extremely competitive offer; and they thought very carefully about how they were going to communicate. A prospective client from the States would certainly have found it all very hard to resist. The trouble was, the prospective clients weren't from the States. They were Mexican. And the Americans failed to take account of that. As a result, they chose the wrong negotiating team; they tried to deal with the Mexicans at the wrong pace and in the wrong place; and they misread the signals that were being sent. This chapter aims to help you avoid making the same costly mistakes.

Picking the right people

Your team

At first sight, you might think that the Americans had selected their team very carefully indeed: there were technical experts who could give a good impression of the company's expertise and answer any difficult questions; lawyers who could negotiate a *watertight* (comprehensive and free from errors) contract; and interpreters who would make sure that everything was communicated clearly and accurately.

So why was this the wrong team for Mexico? Well, as we saw in Chapter 2, not every culture shares the American view that people should be judged solely on what they do. Mexico is a given status culture where other factors such as age and position are also taken into account. The technical experts might have been very knowledgeable, but their level of seniority was way below that of the Mexican minister and his senior officials. So, from the Mexicans' perspective, there was no way they could negotiate on equal terms. To show the kind of respect the Mexicans were expecting, the American team should have been led by a board member, at the very least. As the minister himself was involved, a president, chairman or CEO would probably have been more appropriate – particularly for the initial exchanges.

Including lawyers on the team was another serious mistake. For the Mexicans, business is personal. If you want to make deals with them, you have to build a personal relationship first. Filling the room with lawyers at the very first meeting does little to develop mutual warmth and trust. Why on earth would people who trust each other need lawyers to record and check everything that was being said? Of course, you'll need to bring your lawyers in when you start drawing up the contract. But until then, you should leave them at home.

Some years ago, at the height of the American craze for political correctness in their universities, students were encouraged to sign contractual checklists of what they were and were not willing to do with a potential sexual partner on a first date. That way both partners could be sure they weren't exploiting one another. To much of the rest of the world (and, to be fair, to many Americans), this took all the mystery and romance out of the dating game. It reduced it to a purely functional transaction. Maybe that's what the Mexicans thought the lawyers were doing to the negotiation.

And why did the Americans decide to bring external interpreters with them? Theirs was a huge company with offices all over Latin America. Surely they could have found a Spanish speaker who was in a senior enough position to take an active part in these negotiations. Interpreters are very useful, of course. And there will be some occasions when you have to bring them in. But if you can find someone from within your own organization who speaks the local language, they'll be able to help you get much closer to your partners than an interpreter can. Only one of your own people can show the empathy that is needed to develop a warm and trusting relationship between your two organizations.

The team that the Americans put together reflected their own cultural values. As this was a major infrastructural contract, they assumed that the Mexicans would be interested, above all, in technical expertise, legal guarantees and safeguards, and clear, straightforward communication. But, as we have seen, what the Mexicans were really looking for were partners they could trust; people who showed them warmth and treated them with respect. The team the Americans picked sent all the wrong signals. As a result, they didn't even make it to the negotiating table.

While we're on the subject of picking the right people, we need to say a few words about the role of women. We hear many stories about very able female managers who have been excluded from international teams, or assignments to senior overseas positions, on the grounds of their gender alone. Typically, their head office argues that cultural attitudes in the target country would make it difficult, if not impossible, for a woman to do the job effectively. 'Look at the roles that are defined for their own women', they say. 'There's no way they would accept a female manager of any nationality.' That may be very true of those cultures where men and women are not permitted to mix except inside the home. But there are other apparently male-dominated cultures – Japan, Korea, and indeed Mexico, for example – where a foreign female manager can often do the job just as successfully as a man. Indeed, in some ways, she may even be better suited to the role. No matter where they're headquartered, most business organizations are still male-dominated. And to reach a management position, a woman is likely to need more perseverance, flexibility and networking skills than her male peers. And these are just the kind of qualities that an overseas manager will need.

Our cross cultural consultants have noted, for example, that some of the European and American women working within the Renault–Nissan Alliance tend to benefit from more open communication channels with their Japanese counterparts. As a result, they have sometimes been able to manage difficult situations more effectively than their male peers. And according to our Canning colleagues in Tokyo, the view below – which appeared in *Doing Business with Japanese Men: A Woman's Handbook* (Christalyn Brannen & Tracey Wilen Daugenti, 1993) – is still valid today:

> The greatest advantage I have being a woman is that I can network at many more levels than my male counterparts. In a tightly structured society like Japan's that is much more hierarchical than our own, matching rank or title is very important. Communication happens with your counterpart and you are pretty much confined to network at your own level. It is difficult for a male engineer from my company to talk to an engineer on the Japanese team, for example. Being a woman on business in Japan, however, you are considered something of an oddity and an outsider; so you don't have to observe such strict lines of communication. You must work harder at first to establish yourself as credible, but you can then use your outsider status to your benefit. You can be a very valuable information source for your team because the communication channels from the secretary all the way on up are accessible to you. It is an indispensable negotiating advantage.

Provided her company supports and empowers her, and she herself develops the right strategies to suit the culture she's working in, there's no reason why a woman should not be selected for international assignments, even to countries where women are traditionally subordinate to men.

Their team

Picking the right people for your team is vital. It's equally important to make sure that you are *meeting* the right people.

A very prestigious German company had a long-term relationship with a client firm in North Africa. The firm employed a large team of technical experts with impressive qualifications. And, during the year, the Germans had frequent and successful contact with them.

But when the terms of the contract were renegotiated at the end of every year, these technical experts weren't present. Their president, whose technical expertise was fairly limited, would fly over to Germany on his own and conduct the negotiations himself. That was because his instincts told him that top companies expect to deal with very senior managers. But, of course, for the functional, acquired status Germans, he was the wrong person. They would have been much happier to deal with one of the technical experts. Their annual meetings with the president were a nightmare. They had to explain every single detail to him and it took hours to put the deal together. After one particularly long and frustrating session, the Germans politely suggested that, next time, the president should bring one of his technical experts with him. To their relief, he agreed.

The following year, the Germans arranged for one of their own board members to take care of the president while they negotiated with the technical guy. The president was delighted to be taken to lunch and shown round the company art galleries by someone of his own status. And the Germans were equally delighted to be able to put the deal together so quickly and easily.

Of course, in this case, the two companies already had a long-standing relationship. So meeting the wrong person didn't break the deal. Even so, relations might have deteriorated over time if the Germans hadn't found a way to meet the right person while still showing respect for the president's status. If you meet the wrong person in the initial stages of your relationship, however, the door to that company may be closed to you forever.

When Wim, the managing director of a Dutch tool manufacturer, was looking for a distributor in Asia, he was delighted when Watanabe-san, the chief executive of a major Tokyo firm, agreed to meet him. Wim knew that Japanese corporate structures tended to be much more vertical than in the Netherlands. And so he assumed, logically enough, that the guy at the top of the tree would be the one who made and executed the real decisions. The chief executive's son-in-law, Paul – an Irishman who had worked for the Tokyo firm for many years – acted as interpreter. The meeting was warm and friendly and, as he flew back to Amsterdam, Wim felt very pleased with himself. He was convinced he had found the right business partner. As the weeks passed, however, he heard nothing back from Watanabe-san. Wim tried calling him, but he was never available. He sent him several letters, but they remained unanswered. What had gone wrong? Paul – the Irishman who had acted as interpreter – told us the other side of the story:

> It was really embarrassing. As soon as I walked in, I realized that Watanabe-san wasn't remotely interested in making a deal. You see, he hadn't invited any middle managers to the meeting. And, over here, they're the ones who really put deals together and make them work. But poor old Wim was obviously delighted to be talking to the top guy. As far as he was concerned, that meant the deal was as good as done. For us, it was just a rather meaningless ceremonial discussion between our top man and theirs.

In many parts of the world, a one-to-one meeting with the chief executive would be a very positive signal indeed. But, as we saw in Chapter 2, Japan's business culture is highly group-oriented. Strategic decisions are only taken after a thorough consultation process (*nemawashi*). Your meeting may be with the top man, but if he's the only one who's listening to your pitch, it's highly unlikely to result in a deal.

When you're trying to make a deal with a company whose cultural values are very different from your own, it's not always easy to work out whether the person you're meeting is the right one or not. Our advice, as ever, is to resist the temptation to jump to any hasty conclusions about your prospective partner's motives. Instead, try to read the signals they are sending from their cultural perspective, not yours. If, for example, you're from a group-oriented culture (like Japan, the Arab world or China) and you're doing business with an individualist one (such as the United States, Germany or Britain), don't immediately assume that the deal has no future if there's only one person present at the meeting. As long as you're talking to the right person, there's no reason why the deal shouldn't go ahead.

Similarly, if you're from a given status culture (Latin America, say, or India) and you're meeting someone from an acquired status culture (such as the United States, Australia or the Netherlands), don't be offended if your partner is younger than you, or has a more junior position. She has almost certainly been sent to this negotiation because she has the technical expertise, skills and knowledge to put this particular deal together.

In short, whether you're putting your own team together or evaluating your partners' team, it's vital to make a conscious effort to step outside your own cultural perspectives. As the Americans found to their cost, picking the wrong people can break a deal before you even get to the negotiating table.

Thinking about pace and place

The Americans paid meticulous attention to the schedule and agenda for their presentation and initial meetings with the Mexicans. They also spent a lot of money on the venue. From their perspective, conducting the negotiations at one of the most prestigious hotels in the city had two major advantages: they could offer the Mexicans the kind of top-class hospitality that would obviously be expected; and they would keep control of the negotiating environment. Indeed, their main instinct seems to have been to remain in control; to leave nothing to chance. And to make absolutely sure that nothing would go wrong, they wrote all the arrangements down in great detail and sent them to the Mexican officials well in advance of the meeting.

When they were thinking about pace and place, the Americans assumed that it was vital to demonstrate how serious, well organized and professional they were. As we have seen, this was the wrong assumption to make.

Pace

As we saw in Chapter 1, the Americans are highly monochronic. In their culture, people are judged by how well they can control their time. And people who can't do so are not to be trusted. The Mexicans, on the other hand, are highly polychronic. To them, how you nurture relationships is much more important than how you manage your time. Far from being impressed by the Americans' detailed and carefully timed schedule, the Mexicans probably thought they were being pushy or even arrogant.

The two prospective partners would fall at opposite ends of this scale too:

Speed						Patience				
Too much analysis leads to paralysis.						Taking my time helps me make the right decision.				
50	40	30	20	10	0	10	20	30	40	50

The Mexicans wanted to discuss the proposals among themselves in a leisurely fashion; and they couldn't understand why the Americans were in such a rush. The Americans, on the other hand, were impatient for a decision; they couldn't understand why it was taking the Mexicans so long to consider such a straightforward and attractive offer.

But, of course, the Mexicans weren't simply thinking about the proposals the Americans had made. In fact, they were far more interested in forming an impression of the members of the American team: *Are these the kind of people we want to work with? Can we trust them? Could we build a good relationship with them?* The answer they came to, in each case, was No. And that was largely because, at every stage, the Americans tried to force the pace: they looked anxious and surprised when the Mexicans were late; they started the presentation before the most important person arrived; and they kept reminding the Mexicans of their imminent departure in an attempt to force them to the negotiating table.

When your prospective partners are from a polychronic, patient culture, you won't get anywhere if you tie yourself to self-imposed deadlines or show you are desperate to catch the plane home. You need to allow plenty of time to get to know one another and build the relationship. You have to follow the mood, not the schedule.

When the Mexicans arrived late for the presentation, it was an ideal opportunity for informal and relaxed small talk. The Americans failed to take advantage of this because they were so obsessed with the schedule. For them (as well as the Germans, Swiss and Dutch) time is money. And there's no point in spending too much of either on unproductive small talk. But, as we saw in Chapter 4, for many cultures small talk is an essential part of building or cementing the relationship. So, when you're negotiating internationally, our advice is to follow your partners' lead. And if you come from a culture that is uncomfortable with small talk, make sure you have plenty of open questions ready to use. The more questions you ask, the better you will understand your partners. And that's bound to help you make a better deal.

Communicating clearly across cultures is never easy. So if they had managed to reach the negotiating table, the Americans would certainly have needed an agenda of some kind. But it was a serious mistake to prepare such a rigid agenda without consulting their Mexican partners. An agenda should always be agreed, never imposed. And you need to make sure that you handle it in a way that suits the natural pace and rhythm of the local partner. The linear, timed agenda favoured in monochronic cultures such as the United States and Germany is not universal. In polychronic cultures, like the Arab world, people feel very uncomfortable discussing and finalizing one issue at a time. They tend to take a more circular approach and may well revisit the same point again and again in the course of the meeting. We believe that *nothing is agreed until everything is agreed*; in other words, that successful negotiators link all the issues. In this respect, the way polychronic cultures instinctively handle the agenda can give them a considerable advantage over their more monochronic partners.

American pace is fast by almost any standards. Maybe that's because, perhaps more than any other culture, they embrace change, look constantly to the future, and have little respect for tradition. In fact, they would probably fall to the far left of this scale:

Future						Past				
Tradition gets in the way of progress.						Change needs to respect tradition.				
50	40	30	20	10	0	10	20	30	40	50

The Americans (and other future-oriented cultures like the 'new Russia') tend to see tradition as one of the main barriers to progress. When top Wall Street analyst Byron Wien described Europe as 'an open air museum', he wasn't paying a compliment.

The gap between future- and past-oriented cultures is considerable. While the latter (for example, Europe and Latin America) are likely to focus on problems, the former will be more interested in solutions; while the Americans will be keen to introduce new systems, the Mexicans will be more interested in working out what went wrong with the old ones. These differing perspectives will have a marked impact on the pace of the negotiation and both parties need to be willing to adapt. If you place too much emphasis on the past, the Americans will think you're gloomy, conservative and lacking in dynamism; if you focus exclusively on the future, the Mexicans and Europeans will perceive you as superficial.

It's not just your pace and rhythm that may need to be adapted. You also have to think carefully about *where* your partners expect to conduct the negotiations.

Place

If your colleagues tell you they have just taken part in an international negotiation, what image immediately springs to mind? If you're from a highly functional business culture, you will probably picture the two teams of negotiators facing each other across a conference table in some smart hotel, your company's board room, or the corner of a colleague's office. It's unlikely that you will picture the negotiators sweating in a sauna, sipping malt whiskies in a nightclub, or reclining on sunbeds in the garden of someone's weekend home. But for people from highly personal business cultures, these informal venues are often where the real business takes place.

The Americans naturally assumed that a five star hotel with luxurious conference rooms was the obvious venue for an important international negotiation. But they would have had a much better chance of making a deal if they had been prepared to meet their Mexican partners in a series of more informal, personal settings. Instead of making an attempt to meet them on their own ground, however, they made the Mexicans come to them. The hotel conference room, with all its high-tech equipment flown in from the United States, was an extension of the Americans' territory. They were the rich neighbours and they were going to show their poor relatives how things should be done. At least, that's how the whole arrangement must have appeared to the Mexicans.

The Americans believed that they were acting as attentive and generous hosts and that they were treating their prospective clients as honoured guests. This would have been fine if they had been in the United States. But while they were in Mexico, they should have let the Mexicans play host.

Mexico is a given status culture. That means there are certain protocols that have to be observed when you're dealing with senior people, and behaviour 'onstage' at the negotiating table tends to be fairly formal. In such cultures, it's often more constructive to take the negotiation 'offstage' so that your partners can relax and get to know you. Only then will they feel free to speak frankly and openly.

'Offstage' negotiating can help you get round other problems too – as a French negotiator recently found. He had attended a *Working with the Japanese* course at Canning. A few weeks after the course, he sent us some feedback:

Last month, I took part in a negotiation with our Japanese partners. In the course of the meeting, I asked one of their negotiators a number of questions that related to his area of expertise. But each time, he evaded the question. I was beginning to get very frustrated when I remembered what you had said about taking the negotiations 'offstage'. So I called a break and took this guy into a corner. Once he was away from his colleagues, he happily answered all my questions in full. When we got back to the table, the negotiation started moving again. Going 'offstage' had made an enormous difference.

The Japanese guy wasn't being deliberately obstructive. He just didn't feel comfortable about expressing his opinions in front of so many people. That's because, in his highly group-oriented culture, individuals are not expected to push themselves forward during group meetings. Personal views are usually only exchanged during the informal, one-to-one discussions that take place during *nemawashi*. If the Frenchman had continued asking the same questions again and again – or worse, shown his frustration at the lack of answers – he would have blocked the negotiation and probably damaged the relationship. But because he showed that he understood his Japanese counterpart's difficulties by suggesting a break and having a quiet word with him in the corner, he reinforced the relationship and got the negotiation moving again.

If the Mexican minister had invited the Americans to spend the weekend at his *hacienda*, they might well have been reluctant to accept. As we saw in Chapter 3, fixed truth cultures often regard extravagant entertainment as a form of bribery. Or they may even suspect that their partners are trying to play some kind of dirty trick. That's certainly what our colleague Nigel thought when he met a prospective client in Finland. It was many years ago when he was working as a metals trader for an American investment bank:

> It was my first trip to Finland and I had no idea what to expect. The meeting started at around 11.15 am. I tried to make some small talk, but my counterpart just gave one-word answers to the many questions I asked him. To my surprise, after about 10 minutes, he invited me to have a sauna. Though I was very uncomfortable with the idea, I decided to accept his offer.
>
> We went down to the sauna. Before we went in, we had a beer; we came out of the sauna and had another beer; then another sauna followed by another beer... and so on. Just as my head was beginning to spin, the Finn suddenly started talking business in surprisingly lucid and fluent English. We put a deal together, and I left for the airport. As I waited in the executive lounge, I began to suspect that I had been the victim of a dirty trick: the Finn had got me drunk so that he could lower my defences and get a better deal.
>
> It wasn't until years later that I discovered, during a trip to Finland for Canning, that some Finns can appear cold until they've had a drink and a sauna with you. That's where the relationship is formed. My Finnish client hadn't been playing a dirty trick. He was just trying to be friendly, and had negotiated in good faith.

Nigel's experience is a salutary reminder that people from every culture, no matter how functional their approach to business may appear to be, feel the need to build a relationship with the people they're doing business with; and that even if your negotiating partners seem to fall at the opposite end of the relationship scale from the Mexicans, they may still value the opportunity to get to know you in a more informal setting.

One of the main problems in international negotiations is that one person's dirty trick can be another person's standard negotiating behaviour. The key is to keep an open mind. If you travel the world assuming that all foreigners are trying to play dirty tricks on you, you'll never forge strong international relationships.

For the past few years, we've been asking the participants on our international negotiations courses to fill in a questionnaire about their personal negotiating style. The questions are designed to find out, for example, how important personal relationships are to them, and how important they think they are to their partners. As you might expect, the vast majority – 85 per cent – claim that personal relationships are very important to them; but only 50 per cent believe that they are important to their partners. Our participants come from a very wide cross-section of the world's multinationals and many of those firms deal with each other. So clearly these negotiators are misreading the signals their partners are sending. And differing attitudes to pace and place may well be one of the causes.

Take the American–Mexican deal we've been talking about. The Americans would undoubtedly have claimed that building a personal relationship with their partners was of paramount importance to them. But the Mexicans clearly didn't think that this was the case. And, like 72 per cent of our participants, the Americans would probably also have said that they always look for common ground rather than try to impose a solution on their partners. But, again, the Mexicans would probably have been astonished to hear it.

Your international partners can't read your mind. They can only try to interpret the signals you're sending. And the way they interpret those signals will be strongly influenced by their own cultural norms. The Americans didn't get as far as the negotiating table because the Mexicans were offended by their choice of team and the way they tried to force the pace. Even if you reach the negotiating table, you will still have to work very hard to play the game to win.

Playing the game to win

In our experience, international communication is often of a very low standard. Diplomacy is generally the first casualty; clarity the second. We regularly ask the business people who come on our international negotiations courses to play a game called 'The Prisoners' Dilemma'. Two people are asked to imagine that they're in jail. The trainer – in the role of prison guard – asks each of them, again and again, whether they're prepared to *squeal* (inform) on the other prisoner or not. They're not allowed to communicate with each other. But they know that:

▩ if both of them stay silent, they'll both go free (ie get two points each);

▩ if they both squeal, they'll both go to jail for a very long time (ie get one point each);

▩ if one prisoner talks and the other doesn't, the squealer will be released and given a fat reward (ie three points); his silent partner will be taken out and shot (ie get a zero score).

After each round, the players are told what their fellow prisoner has decided to do. As you would expect, in a mono-cultural group where the two players already know one another, they find it relatively easy to predict how the other is likely to behave in the next round. And they usually fall, fairly quickly, into a pattern of remaining silent. Ultimately, of course, this is what most pairs of prisoners end up doing. But, in a multi-cultural group – particularly where the players don't know each other – it usually takes them much longer to reach that point.

Say, for example, the two players are Renate and Gianni. For the first two rounds they both remain silent. *Here's an opportunity* thinks Gianni. *Renate is obviously a 'sucker'* (someone who is easily deceived). *She's sure to remain silent in the third round, so I'll squeal and claim the reward.* Sure enough, Renate does remain silent in the third round. And when Gianni squeals, she's extremely annoyed. So what does she do in the fourth round? Well, she may bear a *grudge* (feeling of anger or dislike towards someone who has harmed you) and *squeal.* Or she may remain silent in an attempt to teach her cheating partner the right way to behave. If Gianni continues to squeal, however, the game soon deteriorates into a fight to the death. And both players get very low scores.

The analogy between this game and a negotiation is clear. For both players to 'win' they need to trust one another and interpret accurately the signals their partner is sending. When you're negotiating with people from your own or a similar culture, you can usually recognize an aggressive move, a gesture of faith or a capitulation relatively easily. But when your partners are from a different culture, the signals can be much more difficult to read. And if you want to play the game to win, you will need to make a conscious effort to understand what lies behind their behaviour and, of course, to think very carefully about the way you express yourself.

Understanding their beliefs

Clearly, what your partners believe will have a marked impact on how they behave; and, of course, on how they interpret your behaviour.

Chris was running a negotiations course for a group of project leaders – among them Pascale and Bruno – at an engineering firm in France. Pascale's clients were in Austria; Bruno's were in Algeria. Apart from location, the two projects were very similar. They were of an identical size and both were in the public sector. After the initial negotiation, in each case, a written contract had been drawn up. The Austrian document ran to 132 pages; the Algerian one was a mere 7 pages. Out of interest, Chris asked the two project managers how often they actually looked at the contract. Pascale replied that she took the 132-page document with her every time she met her Austrian clients; and that it formed the basis of most of their discussions.

Bruno simply said: 'I took the contract to a meeting in Algeria once. But I'll never make the same mistake again.' Apparently, as soon as he pulled the contract out of his briefcase to clarify a couple of points, his Algerian counterpart exploded: 'Why do you need to look at the contract? If there's a problem, just tell me. And we can find a solution together. I can't believe you're doing this. I thought we trusted each other.' Bruno had to work very hard to get the relationship back on track.

How can something that is accepted as common business practice in Austria cause so much offence in Algeria? Well, part of the answer lies in the two cultures' preferences on the following scale:

Written						Spoken				
For serious issues I prefer the written word.						For serious issues I prefer oral communication.				
50	40	30	20	10	0	10	20	30	40	50

Along with most Northern Europeans and people from the United States, Pascale's Austrian partners would place themselves towards the left of this scale. For them, memoranda of understanding, written summaries and e-mailed offers may carry much more weight than what people say in a meeting; and contracts almost certainly will. That's probably why the Americans took their lawyers to the first meeting with the Mexicans. Bruno's Algerian partner, on the other hand, comes from a culture that has a strong oral tradition. He accepts that contracts are a necessary part of any international deal; but they don't define or shape the relationship as they do in a more written culture.

Before we leave the question of contracts, it's worth pointing out that even in Western Europe, attitudes towards them can vary considerably from country to country.

Our colleague Richard was running a negotiation and communication skills course for a group of project managers from an international IT company. They had just finished role-playing a cross-border, post-contract negotiation. It had gone badly. Richard looked round the room and asked one of the Americans a question: 'What's a contract?' The American, who clearly thought it was a stupid question, replied: 'It defines the deal; it's the Bible.' Massimo from Rome didn't agree: 'A contract is a prison', he said with passion. One of the Frenchmen spoke for a couple of minutes. In short, his message was: 'You have lots of clauses which can be interpreted in different ways'. Meanwhile, the three Dutch guys had been discussing among themselves. One of them said: 'We would call it an insurance document. You only use it if you have to.' The British, who seemed relieved that they didn't have to provide their own answer said: 'We agree with the Dutch.' All of these managers were the same age, worked for the same company and did the same job.

If you lean towards the left of the written–spoken scale and you're trying to make a deal with someone who falls to the right, remember that your partners will probably take what you say more seriously than what you write. So keep the contract out of sight, don't make verbal promises you're not prepared to keep, and beware of taking too many notes. If you spend the whole meeting writing down what they say, they'll think you don't trust them. That's not to say you shouldn't take any notes at all. International negotiation is hard enough, particularly if one or both partners are speaking a language that is not their native tongue. And it's vital to make sure that you've understood one another correctly. But your first priority should be to look at your partners, listen carefully to what they say, and talk to them. If you summarize frequently what has been discussed, you should have no problem remembering the points that have been raised. Summarizing will also enable you to check that you've understood one another correctly. Once something concrete has been agreed, summarize it together verbally, and only then write down a few brief notes.

The Austrians and Algerians would also fall at opposite ends of this scale:

Choice						Destiny				
I am in charge of how I live my life.						Forces beyond my control determine what happens in my life.				
50	40	30	20	10	0	10	20	30	40	50

People from much of North Africa, the Middle East and parts of Asia would place themselves to the right. For them, the black and white certainty of a contract is in conflict with their religious and spiritual beliefs. Forces beyond their control could intervene at any time and disrupt their plans. So how can a document possibly define what will happen in the future? That's probably why the Algerian contract was only seven pages long. If you believe in destiny, there's no point in having a contract that covers every single eventuality. When Muslims are negotiating, they will often qualify what they say with the phrase *Inshallah* (if God wills it). They're not demonstrating an unwillingness to commit to the deal. They're just recognizing that circumstances can change; and reminding you that, if they do, partners who trust each other can always renegotiate the terms of the deal.

When Bruno pulled the contract out of his briefcase, then, his Algerian partner was very offended: partly because it was a signal that Bruno didn't trust him; and partly because it went against his deeply held beliefs about the meaning of life. Fortunately Bruno didn't repeat his mistake. From then on, he left the contract at home and made a conscious effort to show patience and respect for his Algerian partner's beliefs.

All of this is not to say that people from destiny cultures make no attempt to protect their own interests. Far from it. There's an old saying in the Middle East which neatly sums up their approach: *Trust in Allah, but always tie your camel.*

How much importance you attach to the contract isn't the only thing that can send the wrong signals to your partners:

Two firms in the brewing industry, one Dutch and the other Japanese, were in the final stage of negotiating a contract. Neither side was prepared to concede on some minor details. It was Sunday afternoon in one of the Japanese company's breweries. The Dutch team asked for a break and, when offered drinks, requested some beers – they were in a brewery, after all. The Japanese left the room. Instead of the usual 10 minutes, the break lasted nearly an hour. On their return, the leader of the Japanese delegation bowed deeply and said they were now prepared to accept all the remaining demands the Dutch had made. The delighted Dutch and considerably less enthusiastic Japanese shook hands on the deal. Only later did the Dutch discover that their request for alcohol had been interpreted by the Japanese as a subtle: 'Accept our demands or the deal is off.' Traditionally in Japan, alcohol only comes out to celebrate an agreement.

At first sight, this might look like a great result for the Dutch. They accidentally achieved an unexpectedly big 'win'. But there's little point in achieving a result that your partners will struggle to deliver. Which was exactly what happened in this case. The Japanese negotiators had shaken hands on the deal and so, naturally, they signed the contract. But because they had accepted the revised terms without first getting the agreement of each of their colleagues, there were bitter disputes about the concessions they had been forced to make. The Dutch hadn't been trying to cheat on their Japanese partners. But it must have looked that way to many of the Japanese managers who were responsible for executing the deal. As a result – like Renate in 'The Prisoners' Dilemma' – they turned into *grudgers*. And it took the Dutch a long time to regain the trust that was needed for both partners to truly 'win' the game.

If the Dutch could have gone back and changed their drinks order, you can be sure that they would. But you generally only get one chance. And if you send the wrong signal, you could break the deal or cause serious damage to the relationship. So before you do business in an unfamiliar culture, find out about local customs.

Using the right language

It's a pity the Americans in our first case study never got to the negotiating table. If they had, their Mexican partners would most probably have liked them a lot. Earlier in the chapter, we mentioned the global negotiations survey we've been conducting. Another of the questions we ask is: *Who would you most like to be in partnership with?* Interestingly enough, the majority of our participants say that their preferred partners are the Americans or the Germans because: *You know where you are with them. They're direct and they say what they mean.*

As we saw in Chapter 4, the Americans and Germans are low context communicators. So they tend to say what they mean frankly, explicitly and directly. And while they may sometimes be perceived as brusque or aggressive, their transparency makes a welcome change from the confusion and misunderstanding that often *plagues* (troubles) international negotiations.

The least popular negotiating partners, according to our survey, are people from high context cultures (like the British, Italians, Japanese and Arabs). Their lack of clarity seems to confuse and exasperate people. And their partners often assume that they are trying to play dirty tricks on them.

Another interesting statistic is that the Americans seem to be almost twice as popular as the Germans. Maybe that's because they tend to take a more enthusiastic, upbeat and future-oriented approach; and, as we've already seen, they focus on solutions rather than problems. It may also be because they fall to the left of this scale:

Risk-embracing					Risk-averse					
I like taking risks.					I avoid taking risks.					
50	40	30	20	10	0	10	20	30	40	50

Being prepared to take risks means that the Americans rarely react negatively to an innovative proposal. They're more likely to regard it as an opportunity and to be willing to explore the options it presents with an open mind. The Germans, on the other hand, tend to be relatively risk-averse. As we have already seen, they also tend to be more past-focused and to express themselves in a fairly low-key way. As a result, they're likely to spend more time agonizing over problems; and to be less prepared to explore options that could carry too much risk.

Of course, no international business person likes to be thought of as conservative. But judged by American standards, many are. So while the Americans and Germans are both low context communicators, the former may sometimes feel frustrated by the latter's unwillingness to take risks.

As the Germans tend to take a functional approach to business, however, they're very unlikely to resort to deliberate abuse or aggression. Unfortunately, people from some of the more relationship-oriented cultures are sometimes tempted to make comments that are far too personal:

A British businessman was negotiating a large contract in Algeria. After some small talk, he presented his initial offer. His Algerian counterpart reacted very negatively and aggressively. Not only did he reject the proposals outright, but he made some extremely insulting and offensive comments about the Brit's mother and father. Though he was very shocked, the Brit remained calm and waited for the tirade to end. When it finally did, he leaned forward and said: 'Right. So are we ready to negotiate now?' The Algerian smiled: 'I like you', he said. 'I like your style. I think we can do business together.' But, of course, the Brit didn't like the Algerian's style at all. And he did everything he could to avoid doing business with him again.

The Algerian was probably just testing the Brit. And he was doing so in a way that presumably would have been acceptable to partners from his own culture. But using this kind of aggressive and insulting language in the international arena is a serious mistake. Indeed, any attempt to de-stabilize your partners by putting them under unendurable pressure will rarely produce the best deal. The Brit perceived the Algerian guy's personal attack as a dirty trick and he resolved never to do business with him again.

You are bound to feel the need to challenge some of the claims your partners are making, or to reject some of the proposals they're putting on the table. But when you do so, you need to think carefully about the way you're expressing yourself. The most successful international negotiators attack issues, not people. They use language that is clear, direct and explicit while, at the same time, trying to convey a positive and upbeat attitude. That's what the Americans tend to do and, according to our survey, they seem to be the partners that most of our international clients prefer to negotiate with. If you want to follow their example, we recommend you try the three simple techniques below.

Be soft on people, hard on points (SOPHOP)

This is the single most useful piece of advice we can offer to a negotiator who is trying to make deals in the international market. The most fragile aspect in international partnerships is the relationship between the people involved. By maintaining a SOPHOP approach, you should be able to nurture the relationship, while still ensuring that you give no ground on the commercial issues. If your partners have decided that negotiating is about fighting, that's fine. Fight over the points, but do everything in your power to avoid making it personal. Eventually (like the players in 'The Prisoners' Dilemma'), they will follow your example. If you're the one who wants to fight, again, that's OK. But don't let it get personal. Few people in the world will warm to you if you irritate or offend them.

As we've already seen, some cultures treat business as purely functional; for others, it's intensely personal. The latter (for example, people from the Arab world) will often get so emotionally involved that business and personal issues become almost inseparable. So when someone from a functional culture makes what they think is a dispassionate criticism of a business issue, there's a real danger that their relationship-oriented partner will take it personally. To avoid this danger, you need to exercise control over the way you express yourself.

When you want to disagree with someone, or make a comment that may be perceived as negative, avoid the word *you*. That way, it will be clear that you aren't attacking them personally:

Instead of:	*What are **you** going to do about it?*
Say:	*How are **we** going to solve it?*
Instead of:	*I don't agree with **you**.*
Say:	*I'm not sure I agree with **that**.*
Instead of:	*That's not what **you** said before.*
Say:	*Is **that** what we agreed?*

Keep everything conditional

The popularity of American negotiators is based on their ability to explore rather than reject. In other words, they're careful not to close doors or eliminate options too early. Again, it's all down to the language that you use. If, for example, you keep saying *no, can't, don't* or *won't*, a partner who is keen to put together a creative deal will soon become demoralized. The trick is to keep things conditional:

Seller: **If** you place an order for a full year's supply, (**then**) we could cut the price.

Buyer: **If** we ordered a year's supply, (**then**) would you extend the payment period?

Using *If... (then)...* sentences will help you to repackage your partners' proposals, reshape your own shopping list, and keep the deal open – even with a partner who is keen to eliminate possibilities. But you need to be careful how you use words like *will/would, can/could, may/might*; and to be aware that, for example, *place* or *order* will send very different signals from *placed* or *ordered*. Imagine, for example, that early on in the negotiation, the buyer says:

We need delivery in batches of seven hundred units monthly, starting in May.

Which of the two replies below would come most naturally to you?

Seller A: That *gives* us a very short lead time. But we *can* do it if you *pay* for the first batch in advance.

Seller B: That *would* give us a very short lead time. But we *could* do it if you *paid* for the first batch in advance.

In using the present tense – *gives, can* and *pay* – seller A is sending a clear signal that she is able to meet the delivery targets. Seller B, on the other hand, is using the past tense – *would, could* and *paid* – because he wants to explore the options in a more tentative and non-committal way. If you're a native speaker of English, switching between the more tentative, indirect (and sometimes hypothetical) past form and the more decisive, direct (and sometimes pushy) present form will come naturally to you. But you need to remember that non-native speakers often find it hard to distinguish between the two forms. Indeed, when the participants on our language courses discover that English frequently uses the past tense to talk about the future, they're often very surprised. This is particularly true of the Germans.

So if you're a native speaker of English, you will need to make allowances for your non-native-speaking partners. Don't assume that they're deliberately using the more direct present form to send decisive, inflexible or even aggressive signals. If, for example, while you're happily exploring options together, you tentatively ask: *Would you consider extending the payment period?* and they say: *We can't extend the payment period unless you order a full year's supply*, don't assume that they're trying to eliminate this possibility. What they probably mean is: *We might be able to consider extending the payment period if you ordered a full year's supply.* They just don't know how to say it that way.

And if you're a non-native speaker who has not yet mastered this tentative past form, carry on using the present tense but try adding the words *in principle* to your sentence: *Well, in principle, we can extend the payment period if, for example, you order a full year's supply.* That should help you make it clear that you're exploring rather than eliminating options.

Of course, you'll only be able to explore the options properly if you've allowed enough room for movement in your 'bargaining range' – in other words, the gap between your 'entry' and 'exit' points. How wide your partners expect your bargaining range to be will depend on where they come from. It's as foolish to pay the initial asking price for a carpet in Cairo as it is to try to negotiate over the price of a tube of toothpaste in a supermarket in Oslo. If you want the people you're negotiating with to take your bargaining range seriously, make sure that it's culturally credible to them. As a general rule, people from fixed truth cultures tend to keep their bargaining range narrow and may well mistrust you if you move too far from your entry point; people from relative truth cultures, on the other hand, tend to expect a bigger gap between your entry point and target. That's because they regard negotiating as a process to be enjoyed; and trying to close a wide gap gives them a good opportunity to assess their partner's character.

Talk about how you feel

If you keep everything conditional, you should be able to subtly train almost any partner in the world to take a positive, exploratory approach to negotiating. You can help this process further by talking about your feelings, and inviting your partners to do the same. If you use too many closed questions – ones that invite a *Yes* or *No* answer – you'll simply encourage them to reject your proposals. So try to find out how they feel:

Instead of: *Can you accept this price?*

Say: *How do you feel about this price?*

Instead of: *Can you live with a lower margin on this?*

Say: *How would you feel about accepting a lower margin on this?*

By avoiding *Yes* or *No* answers, you give yourself a much better chance of finding room for negotiation.

It doesn't matter whether your partners are given status Mexicans, functional Germans, high context Japanese, reserved Finns, polychronic Arabs, future-focused Russians, logical French, or risk-embracing Americans. You'll only make a successful and lasting deal if you send them the right signals, and interpret the signals they're sending accurately. Being soft on people, hard on points, keeping everything conditional, and talking about how you feel will help you to do that.

Summary

As we mentioned at the beginning of this chapter, it was the Swedes who won the contract with the Mexicans:

The Swedish negotiating team flew to Mexico City a fortnight after the Americans. They, too, had worked very hard to prepare an impressive presentation. But when their friends at the ministry hinted at what had happened with the Americans they decided, at the last moment, to scale their presentation down to a short, formal talk and not to use any high-tech equipment. Their team, which was small, included a board member who spoke Spanish, the head of their Mexican representative office, and their company president. The first meeting with the minister was delayed by two hours. It only lasted 30 minutes and consisted of little more than small talk between the minister, the president and his Spanish-speaking colleagues. The Swedes were then invited to go on a tour of various potential factory sites over the next three days, followed by a day at the minister's *hacienda*. They readily agreed, even though their colleagues had already visited the potential sites at the tender stage. The Swedes had been in Mexico for six days before they were invited to the ministry to make their formal presentation. The minister responded with a speech detailing forcibly where he expected concessions to be made. The president then flew back to Sweden, leaving his team to negotiate the actual deal. Since they had built in quite wide margins on all their costings, the Swedes were happy to trade concessions with the ministry in order to go part of the way towards meeting the minister's demands. Within a month, the Swedish company's president and the minister signed the contract in front of the world's press.

If the monochronic, acquired status, functional Swedes had been the first to meet the Mexicans, they might instinctively have conducted their initial pitch and subsequent conversations in a very similar way to the Americans. Fortunately, they were able to learn from the mistakes their competitors had made. And, even though it meant moving quite a long way from their own cultural preferences, they made a conscious effort to adapt to their more polychronic, given status, relationship-oriented Mexican partners:

- █ **They picked the right people.** Unlike the Americans, they made sure they had people with local knowledge, a senior Spanish speaker, and the president. This made the Mexicans feel comfortable, and showed them the respect they felt they deserved.

- █ **They let the Mexicans set the pace.** They hadn't booked return flights to Sweden. Instead, they were prepared to wait patiently until the Mexicans were ready to see them. And once the negotiations started, they were careful not to impose a tight agenda on the discussions. As a result, the Mexicans were able to relax in the Swedes' company, and to focus on developing a relationship with them.

- █ **They let the Mexicans choose the place.** They happily visited the potential factory sites again, and graciously accepted the minister's invitation to spend the day at his *hacienda*. Away from the formality of the negotiating table, they demonstrated that they could form a partnership, rather than merely sign a contract, with their new Mexican friends.

■ **They played the game to win.** Because they had read the signals correctly they kept their initial presentation short, low-tech and personal. They had built wide margins into their costings so that, when the minister insisted on more favourable terms, they were able to explore ways of trading concessions and reaching a mutually beneficial deal.

In short, they remembered that, in the international arena, it's how you handle the client, above all else, that can make or break a deal.

7 Making yourself understood in English

'No man is exempt from saying silly things; the mischief is to say them deliberately.'

(Michel de Montaigne, *Les Essais'*, bk iii, ch 1, 1588)

Though the previous six chapters have included some tips on using the English language itself, the main focus so far has been on differing styles of communication (high–low context; reserved–effusive, etc.) and how to bridge the gap between them. Now, it's time to look in more detail at ways of making yourself understood in this international lingua franca.

If you're a native English speaker, you might be tempted at this stage to snap the book shut. This chapter can't really be of interest to you, can it? After all, English is your mother tongue. It's all those non-native speakers who have problems making themselves understood, not you. Well no, in fact, that's not really true. In our experience, non-native speakers tend to manage relatively well when they're speaking English amongst themselves; the trouble usually only starts when native speakers – or very fluent non-native speakers like the Dutch or the Swedes – join in.

We recently invited over 400 Canning clients from 26 different nationalities to take part in an opinion survey. While nearly 98 per cent agreed that it's generally a positive thing to be able to communicate with many nationalities in one language (English), the majority prefer doing so with other non-native speakers: in fact, 58 per cent find native speakers more difficult to understand; nearly 56 per cent feel that the effort they're making to operate in a foreign language goes unnoticed by the native speaker; and just under 60 per cent believe that native speakers of English use their linguistic superiority to gain advantage.

The fact that English has become the common language of international business should be very good news for the monolingual American,

Australian, New Zealander or Brit. But, in fact, as we saw in Chapter 6, the native speaker is often at a disadvantage and may even lose business to a non-native speaking competitor whose English can be more easily understood by the customer.

So what is this version of English that non-native speakers use and – it would seem – often prefer? Well, at Canning, we call it *Offshore English* (OE). It's English without the words and expressions that non-native speakers find difficult. It's not beautiful: to the native speaker's ear, it has no subtlety or nuance and can sound plain. But, it does significantly reduce the risk of misunderstanding and confusion in international meetings. Indeed, OE is the true lingua franca of international commerce and to be effective in international groups, the native English speaker has to learn to use it.

If you're a non-native speaker, this is not a signal for you to close the book. Bridging the English language gap requires just as much mutual empathy and effort as overcoming cultural differences. Not only will this chapter show you why using OE doesn't come naturally to your native-speaking business partners, and why they don't seem to notice the efforts you're making to speak their language, it will also give you the opportunity to broaden and refine your own range of English vocabulary and expression.

Though we may occasionally tell you a short anecdote to illustrate the point we're making, we aren't going to base our comments on specific business situations as we have in previous chapters, nor are we going to refer to the cultural preference scales.

Whatever your nationality or native tongue, if you're using English as a lingua franca you have to accept that your version of the language is not the norm. Expressions that you regard as simple may be incomprehensible to people whose first language is different from yours; words whose meaning you've always believed to be universal may have the opposite impact from the one you intended, and your accent which is so easily understood by your compatriots may be very unclear to other nationalities. To become an accomplished OE speaker, you need to do two things: firstly, you need to learn as much as you can about the different ways in which people use the English language, so that you can modify and filter what you say to suit the person you're speaking to, and secondly, you need to adopt some common-sense communication techniques that will help you get your message across with greater clarity, accuracy and warmth.

Language

An international company invited our colleague Gerard Bannon to contribute to the first module of their in-house training programme for high potentials. Though Gerard recommended that his session – on communication – would be most beneficial at the beginning of the five-day module, he had to accept a slot on the last day.

The 32 participants (representing 10 different nationalities) had been working together for four days by the time Gerard met them. As usual, they started with a review of the previous day. It soon became clear that the nine native speakers in the room were monopolizing the discussion. In fact, the 23 non-native speakers were saying almost nothing. When the discussion came to an end, Gerard – who had been making notes – read out some of the expressions that had been used. He asked each of the non-native speakers in the group what these phrases meant. None of them knew. Slightly uncomfortable, but not totally convinced, the native speakers checked with their colleagues directly: 'Do you mean you really don't understand any of those expressions?' The answer was unanimous: 'No, we don't. And we've had the same problem all week'. Two of the Brazilians then stood up and, clearly exasperated, asked: 'Why didn't we have this session on Monday?' It was a reasonable question, but one that only the programme director could answer. So Gerard responded with another equally reasonable question: 'Why has it taken you four days to tell the others you didn't understand them?'

Well, like the majority of people who took part in our survey, the non-native speakers probably thought their colleagues were using their linguistic superiority to gain advantage or, at least, to exclude them from their little native speakers' club. To admit that they didn't understand could make them look stupid; or, worse, invite ridicule or condescension. But the native speakers were clearly shocked – and a little embarrassed – to discover that much of what they had been saying was incomprehensible to their colleagues.

So what kind of language were the native speakers using? And why didn't their colleagues understand it? And how about the non-native speakers? When they finally joined the discussion, did the words and expressions they used always create the impact they intended? Probably not.

Verbs and nouns

As we saw in Chapter 6, native English speakers often automatically choose verbs in preference to nouns. That's just the way the English language works. On the first day of a Canning English for Business course, to check how well our clients understand English, we often ask questions like:

> *Where do you <u>come from?</u>*
> *Who do you <u>work for?</u>*
> *What do you <u>do?</u>*
> *What are you going to <u>do</u> this evening?*

All perfectly standard (and indeed very simple) questions for the native speaker; but not so clear for many of our international clients. Often they look puzzled until we rephrase the questions as follows:

> *Where's your <u>home town?</u>*
> *What's your <u>company?</u>*
> *What's your <u>job?</u>*
> *What's your <u>plan</u> for this evening?*

If you look again at the words that have been underlined, you will see that in the first list, they're all verbs; in the second, they're all nouns.

For a variety of reasons, non-native speakers tend to rely more on nouns than on verbs to get their message across. In some cases, it's because that's what they do in their own language (for example, German and Italian). Most of the time, it's simply because nouns are much easier to learn and simpler to use.

So, if a non-native speaker doesn't understand what you've said, try replacing the verb with a noun:

Instead of: *What are you <u>aiming</u> to achieve?*

say: *What are your <u>objectives?</u>*

Instead of: *John's <u>running</u> the project*

say: *John's the <u>project manager</u>*

Instead of: *Who do you <u>report to?</u>*

say: *Who's your <u>boss?</u>*

And, if you're a non-native speaker and you want your presentation to have more impact on your British and American audience, try to replace some of the nouns you planned to use with verbs.

Latin-based versus Germanic verbs

Of course, we're not saying that non-native speakers never use verbs. But they tend to choose the polysyllabic, Latin-based verbs (for example: *obtain, inform, select, demonstrate*) that are similar to their own language, or that they were taught in school.

> *Did you manage to <u>obtain</u> a copy of the report?*
> *I have to <u>inform</u> you that the price has increased.*
> *<u>Select</u> the one you want.*
> *As I will <u>demonstrate</u> in a minute, this system can help you cut your costs.*

However, these Latin-based verbs often sound too formal – even pedantic – to native speakers, who tend to reserve them for formal written reports. For everyday speech they will generally use a verb (often one-syllable) that comes from the Germanic language stream (for example: *get, tell, pick, show*).

> *Did you manage to <u>get</u> a copy of the report?*
> *I have to <u>tell</u> you that the price has increased.*
> *<u>Pick</u> the one you want.*
> *As I will <u>show</u> you in a minute, this system can help you cut your costs.*

The accomplished OE speaker is able to switch effortlessly between these one-syllable verbs and their Latin-based equivalents. For most native speakers, all this takes is a bit of reflection and practice.

Phrasal verbs

Unfortunately, the difference between OE and native speech doesn't stop there. Have a look at these sentences:

> *When did he <u>get back</u> from Munich?* (return)
> *The delivery is late. You'll have to <u>get on to</u> the suppliers.* (contact)
> *They always pay late. We can't let them <u>get away with</u> it.* (escape without punishment)

It was so embarrassing. He told me off in front of everyone. (reprimanded)

Please don't pick me up from the office. (collect)

You always show me up by wearing that stupid hat. (embarrass/humiliate)

As you can see, each of the verbs (*get, tell, pick, show*) has been combined with other words like *back, on to, away with, off, up* to create a completely new expression. They're what the grammar books call *phrasal verbs*. Native speakers love using phrasal verbs. In fact, to them, phrasal verbs usually sound more natural, normal and easier for people to understand than their Latin-based equivalents (in brackets above). Indeed, when native speakers want to simplify what they're saying, or make it more accessible, they automatically use more and more phrasal verbs.

For most non-native speakers, however (except, perhaps, the Scandinavians, whose own languages have similar structures), phrasal verbs are an absolute nightmare. Most would find the statement below – made by an American commentator on American–Japanese relations – very difficult to understand:

America is no longer prepared to carry on putting up with the obviously unfair trading practices carried out by one of our major trading partners.

In OE, this would be:

America cannot continue to tolerate Japan's unfair trading practices.

If they want to make themselves understood, native speakers need to learn how to replace phrasal verbs with words (verbs or nouns) that are Latin-based or known to be more commonly understood by non-native speakers.

Instead of:	*We'll have to put the meeting off.*
say:	*We'll have to postpone the meeting.*
Instead of:	*The price put me off.*
say:	*The price was a disincentive.*
Instead of:	*Can you get on to him?*

say:	*Can you <u>contact</u> him?*
Instead of:	*Are you <u>getting on</u> OK with the project?*
say:	*Are you <u>making progress</u> with the project?*
Instead of:	*We've <u>come up against</u> a few problems.*
say:	*We've <u>encountered</u> a few problems.*
Instead of:	*He <u>went out of his way</u> to help us.*
say:	*He <u>made a special effort</u> to help us.*

So, is speaking OE just a question of using a few more nouns and switching from phrasal to Latin-based verbs? Well, no, unfortunately not.

False friends

The French and Dutch members of ABC's new post-merger management team were taking part in an 'Optimizing our Teamwork' session run by Canning. At the end, they all agreed that the two bosses – let's call them Olivier and Joop – should issue a 'joint communication' to all the managers in their division, telling them about the new standard operating procedures they had decided to adopt. They were all very happy with this until Richard, their trainer, asked them what they meant by 'joint'. Joop, clearly puzzled by the question, replied: 'Olivier and I will issue an e-mail together with both our names at the bottom. Right, Olivier?' The Frenchman looked unhappy. One of his subordinates spoke for him: 'I think we're proposing to do this in parallel – separately. Each e-mail will say the same things, of course. But we'll do ours in French so that it is clear for everyone.'

Joint is a word that exists in both French and English. Indeed, it comes from the same Latin root. The trouble is, it doesn't always mean the same thing in both languages. To the native speaker – and indeed to Joop – a *joint* e-mail means *one single* e-mail that is *co-authored* by the two parties involved; to the French, it means *separate* but *connected*.

There are a considerable number of words like this in English. For obvious reasons, the French and Germans refer to such words as *false friends* (*faux amis, falsche freunde*). They can cause misunderstanding even among experienced OE speakers. For example:

Word	Meaning to the native speaker	Meaning to many non-native speakers
actually	in fact	now, at the moment
assist	help	attend
benefits	advantages	profits
candid	frank/honest	naive
concurrent	existing or acting at the same time	competitive
eventually	finally	possibly, if the occasion arises
formation	structure/arrangement	training
sympathetic	able to share the emotion of others	nice
a delay	an instance of being late	lead time

In some cases, of course, the false friend applies to only one nationality or language:

The Managing Director of a German company spent all day in London with his local team of British and German managers, discussing the budget for the following year. They couldn't agree on what percentage should be allocated to 'provisions'. The Brits felt that 5 per cent was more than enough; the Germans thought it should be no less than 10 per cent. At the end of a very frustrating day, the German MD asked: 'What exactly do you mean by provisions?'

If he had asked the question at the beginning of the day, he could have saved a lot of time and frustration. To the Germans, *provisions* meant commission for the sales team; to the Brits it meant a contingency for any unexpected expenditure.

And if a native Spanish speaker asks you whether you have your carpet (*carpeta*), she will probably be referring to your file or folder. But if something went badly wrong during her presentation, she's unlikely to tell you that she was embarrassed as *embarazada* means pregnant.

If an Italian says he would like you to anticipate (*anticipare*) the meeting, he isn't asking you to think about it in advance; he wants you to *bring it forward* (move it to an earlier date or time).

Though there are examples of false friends from many languages, by far the most confusion is caused by words that come from Latin. For a fuller list, have a look at the Appendix on page 185.

Experienced OE speakers build up their knowledge of false friends over time by listening carefully and checking anything that sounds ambiguous or unclear: *Sorry, when you say you can't actually help us, what do you mean?*

British and American usage

One of Chris Fox's American clients – a large pharmaceutical company – asked him to send over a 'high level proposal' for speaker training at a big marketing event. Chris took this to mean they wanted a document that would impress their senior decision makers. So he spent a long time producing a comprehensive proposal with plenty of detail about the programme he proposed to run. As soon as his clients received it, they e-mailed back and asked Chris why he hadn't sent them a 'high level proposal' as they had requested. It turned out that by 'high level' they meant a rough outline (as seen from on high) with very little detail – the opposite of what Chris had understood.

The British and the Americans have been described as *two nations divided by a common language*. As we've already seen (Chapter 4), one of the reasons for this division is that Americans tend to be relatively low context communicators, while the British are relatively high context.

As Chris's experience illustrates, the language the two nations have in common is often used to mean very different things too. Indeed, some words and expressions could be described as *false friends*, for they mean one thing to the Americans and something completely different to the British. Below are just a few examples:

Word or expression	Meaning to Americans	Meaning to the British
presently	at the present time	soon
momentarily	very soon	for a brief moment
to slate	to schedule	to denigrate
I'm not with you	I don't support you	I don't understand you
sanctioned	prohibited	approved

'High level proposal' was an expression that Chris wasn't familiar with. Of course, he knew what *high level* meant and he knew what a *proposal* was. But he had never heard this combination of words (or collocation) before. Though he's an experienced and accomplished OE speaker, he didn't ask the clients what they meant. Instead, he made an assumption which gave him a lot of unnecessary work and put him at risk of irritating the client. We can all learn from his mistake.

Please and must

Though these two words are not in exactly the same category as false friends, non-native speakers are often unaware of the negative impact they may have on native speakers:

Please

Most non-native speakers of English imagine that this is a magic word, essential for everyday good manners and pleasantness. And so it is – up to a point. But it isn't the universal panacea they think it is. In fact, *please* can often be autocratic or official. *Please do not walk on the grass* isn't a request, it's a bureaucratic instruction. And if you use this kind of imperative too frequently, you could give native speakers the wrong impression.

The basic 'ask me nicely' words that native speakers learn at their mother's knee are *can/could, will/would*. The word *please* is often an optional extra, and normally appears at the end of the phrase rather than the beginning.

So instead of: *Please do it now.*

say: *Can you do it now (please)?*

Instead of: *Please send me a copy of the report.*

say: *Will you send me a copy of the report (please)?*

Instead of: *Please connect me to Mr Smith.*

say: *Could you connect me to Mr Smith (please)?*

Must

This is another word that, to native speakers, often conveys a bureaucratic or peremptory tone:

You must return your completed form to this office by 30 November.

It's particularly hard for non-native speakers of English to be sure of the precise impact that words like *must, need, have to, should* are likely to have. This may be because their own languages express obligation, necessity and strong recommendation in a completely different way from English; or it may be because they have similar words in their own language that are false friends. In German, for example, the word *müssen* is far less dictatorial than *must*. So if a German says:

You must work this Saturday.
You must send me your report on the fifth day of the month.
We must meet at the office at 8.30.

he probably means:

I'm afraid you're going to have to work this Saturday.
I need to have your report on the fifth day of the month.
I suggest we meet at the office at 8.30.

A lot of non-native speakers also have problems using the negative form of *must* and this can lead to considerable confusion. When non-native speakers say:

> *You mustn't wear a tie to the theatre in London.*
> *They mustn't deliver the parts this week.*
> *She mustn't call the suppliers today.*

what they usually mean is:

> *You don't have to wear a tie to the theatre in London.*
> *They don't have to deliver the parts this week.*
> *She doesn't have to call the suppliers today.*

In other words, if she wants to do it she can, but it's not compulsory.

And just to complicate matters even further, if your French colleagues say:

> *You have not to discuss this with your team until the decision is finalized.*

they mean:

> *You mustn't* (Could I ask you not to) *discuss this with your team until the decision is finalized.*

OK

You would think there was absolutely no scope for misunderstanding with this universal signal of agreement or approval. But unfortunately, in some contexts, OK means different things to different people.

Imagine you have just spent five days away from home on a training course. The host family you stayed with were warm and welcoming and your room was very comfortable. The course itself exceeded your expectations in every way. So when you come to fill in the course evaluation, how do you describe the programme, the trainers, the host family? Do you say they were *excellent* or *very good*; or do you simply put *OK* against every question?

To the native speaker, OK in this context means *satisfactory* or *acceptable* – but no more than that. In the United Kingdom, it's what we would call *faint praise* (weak approval). To describe the course or the host family as *OK* is so lacking in enthusiasm that it implies a certain dissatisfaction or disapproval. And most Brits would want to ask: So *what was wrong with it? What didn't you like?*

To many non-native speakers, however, *OK* doesn't have this potentially negative connotation. It means *absolutely fine; nothing at all to complain about.* Even though our Canning trainers and host families know this, we still feel slightly deflated when one of our clients describes everything as simply *OK*.

Idioms

An idiom is a group of words whose meaning has been established by usage and can't be deduced from the meaning of the individual words:

It's a question of swings and roundabouts. (The two options are very similar.)
It's all gone pear-shaped. (Everything has gone wrong, we have failed.)
His reaction was a bit over the top. (His reaction was excessive/unreasonable.)
He's throwing a sickie. (He's pretending to be ill so that he can take time off work.)
I'm out of here. (I'm leaving.)
He damned it with faint praise. (He commended it so unenthusiastically that he implied disapproval – see OK above.)

For the non-native speaker, these turns of phrase are extremely difficult to understand or translate. And even if a similar expression exists in several languages, you can never guarantee that it will have the same meaning:

When Richard Pooley was working as a VSO teacher in Botswana in the early 1970s, Edith – a 60-year old female colleague – told him she had received some good news from her home in Canada. Richard mentioned this to his pupils and told them that Edith was 'over the moon'. At the end of the class, they all ran over to Edith, congratulated her on this 'miracle from God' and asked her if she was hoping for a baby boy or a baby girl.

In English, *over the moon* means *very happy* or *delighted*. In Setswana, a woman who 'jumps the moon' is pregnant.

Idioms come into and go out of fashion and are often country, or even region, specific. Many British idioms are unintelligible to Americans – and vice versa. So if you want to make yourself understood in English, it's probably best to try and avoid using idioms wherever you can.

Communication techniques

Whatever your native tongue, making yourself understood in English requires conscious effort, sensitivity and a lot of goodwill. There's no doubt that some people find it easier to do than others. Very occasionally, we meet people who simply don't accept the need to modify their language at all. This is how a British manager on one of our courses reacted to the idea of speaking OE:

> That's completely OTT. All you need to do is set your stall out as you meant to go. There's no need for all this pussyfooting around. All you end up with is a completely stilted form of communication.

Hmm, very easy to understand. In fact, in his exasperation, he mixed his idioms and his metaphors so inarticulately that his precise meaning isn't clear, even to a fellow Brit. But the general message is very clear:

> It's completely unreasonable. All you need to do is say exactly what you mean. It's totally unnecessary to speak in such a careful and hypocritical way. The end result will be a completely unnatural and artificial form of communication.

It may seem an unreasonable and even arrogant reaction. But the way you speak is closely linked to your own identity. And the impression you form of others is often influenced as much by the language they use as by the actual ideas they express. This is why some people can feel threatened if they're asked to adopt words and expressions they don't normally use. Like the British manager above, they assume that speaking OE means being hypocritical or false.

As we saw in Chapter 4, some of the non-native speakers on our English for Business courses react in an equally indignant way when they first hear some of the indirect turns of phrase that come naturally to the relatively high context Brits. They translate these phrases literally into their own language and then assume that the native speaker is being hypocritical or dishonest. And they certainly don't want to adopt these turns of phrase themselves. This is particularly true of low context communicators like the Germans and Scandinavians. When, for example, we gently suggest that: *I'm afraid you're going to have to work this Saturday* might have a more positive impact on George than *You must work this Saturday*, they express the same objections as the British manager did.

So the first obstacle you have to overcome is yourself. Speaking OE doesn't mean changing your personality or saying anything you don't believe. All you have to do is exercise a bit of control over the words and expressions you use. It won't make you appear foolish or artificial. Quite the reverse: it will help you to show consideration and respect for people from other cultures and to communicate with them more successfully. Indeed, in our experience, making a conscious effort to speak OE is one of the most effective ways of creating a positive atmosphere when different nationalities come together.

With practice, you will become gradually more proficient at speaking OE. And the more proficient you become, the more comfortable you will feel. But, clearly, you will never be able to predict and avoid every area of potential confusion. That's why the successful OE speaker also adopts some common-sense communication techniques (many have already been mentioned in previous chapters) to help them achieve greater clarity, accuracy and warmth.

Be observant

The nine native speakers in Gerard's communication session weren't unwilling to modify their language. They simply had no idea that the idioms they were using were so incomprehensible. The question is, why didn't they notice that the 23 non-native speakers were contributing almost nothing to the conversation? Well, it was a stimulating, fast-moving discussion, they were making jokes and having fun. They probably didn't even look at the people who weren't taking an active part.

But this is just the kind of situation that gives native speakers a bad reputation. If the nine colleagues had been more observant, they would have realized that something was wrong. So keep your eyes and ears open. If you see that some people are not taking part in the discussion, make a conscious effort to involve them.

Interrupt when you don't understand

Of course, many native speakers will find it equally hard to understand why the 23 non-native speakers sat there for four days without saying anything. But if you're a non-native speaker, you probably know exactly how they felt. In fact, you've probably found yourself in a similar situation: the discussion went too fast; you couldn't follow exactly what the native speakers were saying; and even when you did understand, it took you several seconds to formulate a reply; and by then, the conversation had moved on.

But you've taken the trouble to learn their language. It's their responsibility to help you as much as they can. So interrupt them. Tell them you don't understand. They're the ones who should feel embarrassed if you can't follow them. Not you.

Check and clarify

As Chris's misunderstanding of *high level proposal* illustrates, even the most accomplished OE speakers encounter turns of phrase that take them by surprise. Chris wasn't familiar with the expression the Americans used; nor were his Canning colleagues. So why didn't he simply e-mail his clients and ask them what they meant? Well, the truth is he felt slightly embarrassed. What would the Americans think of an international communications consultant who didn't know what a high level proposal was? So he made an assumption. He and his Canning colleagues agreed that it must mean a detailed and polished report designed for senior decision makers. But this assumption was based on British usage. And, as Chris discovered to his cost, it was completely wrong.

If you have any doubts about what your colleagues have said or written, don't wait and hope that the meaning will become clear later. Ask them for clarification straight away:

> *Sorry, I'm not familiar with that expression. What do you mean by 'high level proposal'?*
> *Sorry, can I check that?*
> *When you say 'eventually', what do you mean?*
> *Does that mean 'finally' or 'possibly'?*
> *Are you saying that you can't meet the deadline?*

And regularly check that others have understood what you have said:

> *Is that clear?*
> *Do you understand what I mean?*

Double check letters, numbers, dates and times

Letters

> At a meeting between Japanese and French managers, ten options (A to J) were discussed. It was agreed that both groups should go ahead and work on Option G. Some months later, they discovered that while the Japanese group had indeed been working on Option G, the French had been working on Option J.

The French – and most of the rest of western Europe – may use the same alphabet as the Americans and the British. But they certainly don't pronounce the letters in the same way. In fact, *g* and *j* could be described as false friends: the French pronounce *g* as *j* and *j* as *g*.

These are not the only letters that can cause confusion. When the French (and other Romance language speakers) see *i* they say *e*; and when they see *a* they say something that sounds like *r* (ah).

So if you want to avoid costly or embarrassing mistakes, don't rely on the spoken word alone. Double check by writing the letter on a notepad or flipchart.

And, avoid acronyms like EFL (English as a Foreign Language) and TUC (Trades Union Congress) – unless they're part of your in-house jargon and you're absolutely sure that everyone around the table is familiar with them.

Numbers and dates

However fluent non-native English speakers may be, they will nearly always resort to their mother tongue to do calculations. How people count varies considerably from language to language. The Japanese, for example, describe high numbers as multiples of 10,000 (*man*), so 100,000 is 10 × 10,000 (*juman*). And the French describe 70 as 60-10 (*soixante-dix*), 80 as 4 × 20 (*quatre-vingts*) and 99 as 4 × 20 + 19 (*quatre-vingt-dix-neuf*).

So when you're speaking OE, don't just say: *We made three hundred and twenty-three thousand dollars* or *The company was set up in nineteen ninety-five*. Write the numbers and dates down. And if you're making a presentation, show them on a slide.

Times

A German businessman was following a two-week Canning English for Business course in preparation for relocating to London. At the weekend, he planned to look for an apartment to rent. The estate agent had arranged to meet him outside one of the apartments he wanted to view at 'half nine'. The German arrived at 8.30, waited till just after 9.00 and then returned to his hotel, furious at the agent's failure to keep their appointment. Meanwhile, the agent arrived punctually at 9.30, waited ten minutes and then called the German to find out where he was.

When Brits say *half nine*, they mean 9.30. But, as you've probably guessed, to native German speakers *halb neun* (literally *half nine*) means 8.30. And it isn't only the Germans who have problems understanding what time of day the Brits are talking about. Many non-native speakers find expressions like: *a quarter to 10*, or *twenty-five past eleven* hard to catch. They will probably understand you better if you speak like a railway timetable:

Instead of: *half past nine or half nine*

say: *nine thirty*

Instead of: *a quarter to ten*

say: *nine forty-five*

It's probably a good idea, too, to avoid using *am* and *pm*.

Instead of: *seven fifteen pm*

say: *nineteen fifteen*

And you may also need to clarify that *fifteen is one five* (15) as opposed to *five zero* (50). When you and your colleagues are speaking OE, differences in pronunciation can make it difficult for both native and non-native speakers to hear the difference between the 'teens' (13 to 19) and the 'tens' (30 to 90).

So again, if there is any doubt, write the time down. It could save a lot of frustration.

Avoid long complicated sentences

Long complicated sentences, which can go on forever, making it very diffi-cult, if not impossible, for the poor listener, who is already straining to grasp the meaning of what you are saying, to remember how your sentence began, should be avoided at all costs.

To be a successful OE speaker, you need to:

■ keep your sentences short and simple;

■ restrict yourself to one idea per sentence.

Think clearly about the words you use and the message you're trying to convey

Some years ago, our colleague Nigel attended an internal management meeting at the Tokyo office of a large German pharmaceutical company. A senior German manager (G) made a short presentation to introduce the Japanese team to the company's 'Management by Objectives' (MBO) system. At the end of the presentation, one of the Japanese managers (J) asked the meaning of 'objective'. Clearly disappointed by J's apparently low level of English, G began to explain as slowly and clearly as he could:

G: *An objective in MBO is an agreed aim or goal.*

J: So aim, goal and objective have the same meaning?

G: *Basically, yes. But in MBO, the objective should be measurable.*

J: Ah, so it's like a budget.

G: *Not really. The budget is a quantitative target. Objectives can be qualitative targets too.*

J: So target means the same as objective?

G: *Basically yes. You see, it's not enough just to have goals. In MBO, you need to agree your objectives as commitments; and then to set even more ambitious targets in order to meet the overall strategic aims of the company.*

The meeting ended in confusion.

The words *objective, aim, goal, target* are synonyms. In other words, in many contexts, they have exactly or nearly the same meaning: something that you want to achieve, the object of your efforts or ambition, the point or result you're trying to reach. People often use synonyms to avoid sounding repetitive and to add clarity or emphasis to what they're saying. At first sight, that's what the German manager appears to be doing. But if you look more closely, you will see that his use of synonyms actually distracts the listener from the message he's trying to convey. Particularly for his Japanese colleagues who assumed that *aim, goal* and *target* must have very specific meanings of which they were unaware. Once you replace all the synonyms G has used with the word *objective*, it may be inelegant, but the message is much clearer:

> G: *An objective in MBO is an <u>agreed</u> objective.*
> *The objective should be <u>measurable</u>.*
> *It can be <u>qualitative</u> as well as <u>quantitative</u>.*
> *It's not enough just to <u>have</u> objectives. In MBO, you need to <u>agree</u> your objectives as <u>commitments</u>; and then to set even <u>more ambitious</u> objectives in order to meet the <u>overall strategic</u> objectives of the company.*

In this version, the emphasis shifts to the underlined words and these are the words that explain what objective means in the context of MBO, which is clearly what was puzzling his Japanese colleague. An experienced OE speaker would have thought in advance about the questions his colleagues were likely to have; and then formulated his message and chosen his words with greater care.

Signpost and summarise

Help your partners follow what you're saying by signposting and summarizing:

Signposting

Make explicit the fact that you are, for example, asking a question, changing subject, referring back to a previous point:

> *Can I ask you a question?*
> *Moving on to the second option...*
> *As I was saying earlier...*

Summarizing

When you're speaking OE, you need to summarise often. At a meeting, do so at regular intervals and particularly before moving to a new point on the agenda. This will help you check that there has been no misunderstanding and that everyone is clear on what action should now be taken and by whom:

> *Before we move on, let's summarise what we have agreed so far...*
> *So, if I've understood correctly, there are three action points...*

Speak clearly

There's no denying that differing pronunciations and speech rhythms can cause considerable comprehension problems for the international English speaker. But it's very difficult for native or non-native speakers of English to change the accent or speech rhythms that come naturally to them. And we're not even going to suggest that you try.

But there are some relatively easy steps you can take that will help others understand you better.

Control your speed

Speaking too *fast* is the most common mistake. If you speak too *slowly*, however, you could sound artificial, monotonous or even patronizing. It may even make it more difficult for others to understand you. That's because when you speak very slowly, you generally pause after each word. And the natural emphasis of each phrase or sentence – which usually helps listeners predict or grasp blocks of meaning – is lost. The secret is to enunciate the words in each phrase or sentence clearly, but at normal speed and with a natural rhythm. Then pause.

Pause after a phrase or sentence, not after each word

Pause for one or two beats at the end of a phrase and for three or four beats at the end of a sentence. For example:

As I was saying earlier (one, two), *we need to make several changes* (one) *to the specification* (one, two, three, four). *The reason for this* (one, two) *is the new European legislation* (one, two, three). *As you probably know* (one, two)...

These pauses will give your listeners time to absorb what you're saying. Pausing will also give you time to think about the language you're using. And this will help you to avoid the words and expressions that your colleagues may not understand.

Control your volume

Some people naturally speak more softly than others. We're not suggesting that you adopt a volume that feels or sounds unnatural. But if you're speaking at an international meeting, look around the table. Are your partners leaning forward, frowning and turning one ear towards you? If they are, it's probably because either they can't hear you, or they can't understand what you're saying. So check: *Can you hear me?*

If they can't, it may be because you're speaking too softly. Often it will be because you're looking down or dropping your voice at the end of a sentence. If you look up and keep your volume constant, people will find it much easier to catch what you're saying, even if you're speaking relatively softly.

Give your colleagues time to tune in to your accent

It's often a good idea to give people time to become accustomed to your accent and the way you speak. So in a presentation, try to make your introduction slightly longer than usual; at a meeting, try to spend a little more time on the small talk.

Remember the human element

As we have already mentioned, OE delivers the message in a concrete, direct and unequivocal fashion:

> *You'll have to change the specification*
> *I don't agree...*
> *I can't do that...*

That doesn't mean it should sound like a conversation between two robots. In your efforts to be clear and concrete, don't forget the human element. Remember to use short expressions like:

> *I appreciate that...*
> *I know this will be difficult for you...*
> *I'm sorry but...*

that humanize the conversation, soften a tough message, or simply acknowledge the relationship.

And try to avoid speaking in a monotone. This doesn't only make it harder for people to understand you; it also makes you sound cold and uninterested. Try to inject warmth into your voice; often a smile is the most effective way to do this.

Control your body language

Researchers tell us that around 60 per cent of communication is non-verbal. As we saw in Chapter 4, people will judge you as much by what your arms, head and eyes are doing as by what you're saying. So keep control of your body as well as your language. Adopt a posture that is open and relaxed, yet dignified; use hand gestures that are expressive, but controlled.

And be aware of what the local culture feels about eye contact, personal space and touching. As always, adapt what you do to the expectations of the culture you're dealing with.

Summary

Acquiring the ability to convey complex ideas in simple, accessible words and sentences – in other words, learning how to speak OE – can be hard work, particularly for native speakers. It requires self-control, clarity of thought and a conscious effort of will. But it's a vital skill if you want to communicate more effectively and success-fully with your international counterparts. Speaking OE won't make you appear hypocritical, false or foolish. You don't have to be untrue to yourself, or say anything that you don't believe. You just have to modify and filter what you say to suit the needs of the person you're speaking to; and adopt some common-sense commu-nication techniques that will reinforce the clarity and accuracy of your message and the warmth of the relationship.

Language

Accept that your version of English is not the norm. If your counter-part looks puzzled or surprised:

- Use a noun instead of a verb.

- Replace a verb of Germanic origin with a Latin-based verb or noun.

- Avoid using too many phrasal verbs.

- Check that the word you have used isn't a false friend.

- Remember that the Americans and British often use their common language to mean different things.

- Remember that *please, must* and *OK* mean different things to different people.

- Avoid using idioms.

Communication techniques

■ Be observant: if you see that some people aren't taking part in the discussion, make a conscious effort to involve them.

■ Don't sit in silence if you can't follow the conversation; interrupt and ask your counterparts to slow down.

■ If in any doubt, check and clarify the meaning of what has been said or written.

■ Double-check your understanding of any letters, numbers, dates or times by writing them down.

■ Avoid long complicated sentences.

■ Think clearly about the words you're using and the message you want to convey.

■ Signpost and summarize frequently.

■ Speak as clearly as you can by controlling your speed, pausing after a phrase or sentence, and controlling your volume.

■ Use phrases and expressions that recognize the relationship and humanize what you're saying.

■ Control your body language.

8 Knowing yourself

Know then thyself, presume not God to scan;
The proper study of mankind is man.

(Alexander Pope, English poet, 1688–1744)

Most of the misunderstandings we described in the first six chapters arose because the people involved wrongly assumed that their own beliefs and attitudes were normal. In many cases, they probably assumed that their own version of English was universal, too. Clearly, OE is an important tool when you're communicating internationally. Not only will it help you make yourself understood, it will also enable you to establish an atmosphere of respect and consideration. And that, in turn, will make it easier for you to recognize any culture gaps there may be.

We believe that knowing yourself is the first and most important step towards bridging the culture gap. The second is to acknowledge that the way you and your compatriots look at the world is not universal. The third is to find out as much as you can about what other cultures value and what lies behind their beliefs. That's why we asked you to place yourself and people from differing cultures on a series of preference scales.

In this chapter, we invite you to look at all those scales again. To help you focus your mind on the key issues, we've grouped them under five main headings: relationships, communication, time, truth, and the meaning of life. What people expect of presenters is informed by their attitudes towards these key issues. But, for ease of reference, we've grouped the presentation style scales together at the end. After each set of scales, you'll find some simple tips – most of which have already appeared in the previous chapters – on how you could adapt your style when you're doing business with people whose preferences are very different from your own.

There are, of course, no magic formulae. No two cultures, or indeed individuals, are exactly the same. The number of variables is infinite. So there's no way that something as two-dimensional as the preference scales can provide you with a comprehensive and totally accurate model of your own or any other culture. But that is not their aim. They're simply there to draw your attention to some of the differences that, in our experience, exist from one culture to another. And to help you start the long process of building your own cultural models through research, observation, and objective analysis.

Similarly, human behaviour is complex and subtle. No one can do it justice in a simple list of DOs and DON'Ts. The tips we offer are necessarily very general. And, taken individually, some of them may seem very obvious to you. Again, they're just there as a starting point; to remind you that the way you do things in your part of the world is not necessarily universal.

When you look at the scales below, remember to examine each pair of statements in relation to your *working* life. Ask yourself what you personally value and try to achieve whenever possible. Then mark, only once, where your instinctive preference falls.

Relationships

Individualist						Group-oriented				
My first duty should be to myself.						My first duty should be to the group I belong to.				
50	40	30	20	10	0	10	20	30	40	50

Flat hierarchy						Vertical hierarchy				
Leaders should share power.						Leaders should hold power.				
50	40	30	20	10	0	10	20	30	40	50

Acquired status						Given status				
People should be judged on what they do, not who they are.						Other factors – such as family, class, nationality, race, education, age, sex, religion – should also be taken into account.				
50	40	30	20	10	0	10	20	30	40	50

Functional						Personal				
We need to focus on business first and personal relationships later in order to do successful business.						We need to build a personal relationship first in order to do successful business.				
50	40	30	20	10	0	10	20	30	40	50

Physically distant						Physically close				
I prefer people not to come too close to me physically.						I think physical closeness and touch are reassuring.				
50	40	30	20	10	0	10	20	30	40	50

Individualist–group-oriented

People from individualist cultures like the Americans, British, Dutch, Northern Italians and French tend to take personal responsibility for their own career development. They focus on the tasks set out in their job description and think it's normal for a boss to reward individual effort with public praise or rapid promotion. If something goes wrong – for example, a deadline is missed, or a mistake is made – they tend to give the reasons why rather than simply apologize. When you're doing business with someone from an individualist culture, you need to:

■ Introduce yourself with confidence.

■ Be prepared to state your own views forcibly and eloquently.

■ Be prepared to challenge what people say.

Most Asian, Arab and African cultures are highly group-oriented. People tend to subordinate their personal goals to those of the group they belong to. And they often try to avoid open conflict with other group members. In Japan, for example, harmony must be preserved at all costs: *If somebody conflicts with others and is excluded from the community, he cannot survive. No prima donnas are welcomed.* When your business partner comes from a highly group-oriented culture, you should:

■ Introduce yourself in relation to your company or team.
The card-exchange ritual so prevalent in many Asian cultures will help you do this. The information on the card puts you, the individual, in the context of the company or group.

■ Talk early on about their company.

■ Speak calmly and slowly, matching the pace of the discussion.

■ Be ready to negotiate with and as part of a large team.
If you do business alone, you'll send negative messages. Not only does it lower your status, it insults your hosts – as it implies they are worth only one person. It also means they can't evaluate the effectiveness of your company's teamwork, a vital skill in any group-oriented culture.

■ Be prepared to do the real business over a meal or in the bar.
Group meetings in many cultures are simply to exchange information or to confirm decisions. If you want your Korean, Japanese or Chinese partners to make concessions or explain a problem, this is often best done one-to-one away from the group. That way, there's no danger of public loss of face.

Flat hierarchy–vertical hierarchy

People from Scandinavia and Australia would probably fall to the far left of this scale (remember the 'Jante Law' and 'Tall Poppy Syndrome'). In Germany, Switzerland, the Netherlands, the United Kingdom and the United States, company hierarchies are also relatively flat. Bosses tend to consult widely, and subordinates generally feel free to express their own views and challenge their boss's decisions. People from flat cultures expect you to:

■ **Take full responsibility for your area of expertise.**
Subordinates openly disagree and argue with their seniors. Such debate is regarded as healthy and likely to lead to good decisions.

■ **Tackle colleagues directly if there's a problem.**
If you run to the boss every time a colleague is being difficult, you'll make yourself very unpopular.

In France, Spain, Italy, Latin America, South-East Asia, India, China, Africa and the Arab world, power in companies is held by a few people at the top. And managers are expected to tell people what to do. When the people you're doing business with come from one of these vertical cultures, you need to:

■ **Have clear lines of communication to senior management.**
Apart from Japan, where consensus (*nemawashi*) is the norm, decisions tend to be made by a small group, or one person, at the very top. You must have their/his (sadly, seldom her) ear.

■ **Keep valuable information to yourself.**
Only share it with those who can help you. Those *in the know* are much admired.

■ **Show a great deal of respect to the decision-makers.**
Avoid flattery, though. They will respect you if you demonstrate quick-wittedness and creativity. Don't get angry if your best ideas somehow become the brilliant solutions of the company president.

■ **Be autocratic in your dealings with subordinates.**
If you're a manager from a flat culture, you will find this very hard; but you must do it. If you seek the opinions of juniors, they will often simply tell you what they think you want to hear. Tell them firmly what you want done. Then watch and listen very carefully to see whether your demand is feasible or not. In many

vertical cultures, senior people will have secretaries or assistants whose most important, but unstated, task is to tell the boss where he's going wrong. You should cultivate these people.

Acquired status–given status

The idea that businesses should be run along meritocratic lines is becoming more common. And many people would, at first sight, place themselves to the left of this scale. There are, nonetheless, many cultures that lean towards the right. Among them are Spain, Southern Italy, South America, India, China, Japan, the Arab world and Africa. In given status cultures, how fast you work your way up the hierarchy doesn't just depend on how well you perform. Factors like age, gender, social status and educational background are also taken into consideration. And managers often behave in a paternalistic way. When you're dealing with people from the given status end of the scale, you should:

■ **Show respect for those older than you.**
This is true whatever their official position. Respect is often shown through body language. In many parts of Africa, for example, when you shake hands with someone older, you take the lower part of his right arm with your left hand.

■ **Consider the age and length of service of your staff when assigning jobs.**
A young person who has not worked long for your company may have all the technical skills, but they will still not be taken seriously in most Asian, African and Arab cultures. Take this into account when you're choosing the members of your negotiating team or the new manager for an overseas operation.

■ **Be paternalistic with your subordinates.**
This is difficult for people from an acquired status culture. But you will be expected to look after your juniors: champion them for promotion or the best jobs, protect them in intra-company disputes, and advise them on personal matters. Much of a manager's time in Asian cultures is spent attending the weddings and funerals of his juniors' families, acting as a marriage arranger, dispensing financial advice, and giving direct on-the-job training. As an outsider, you can't do all these things. But try to have plenty of one-to-one meetings with your subordinates where the discussion is largely about their personal lives. It may be small talk to you, but it will gain you their loyalty.

And if you're a woman, you may have to work harder than your male counterparts to establish your status and credentials:

■ **Dress appropriately**
Bare legs, short skirts and low necklines may be perfectly acceptable in London, Paris or Rome, but they could create the wrong impression elsewhere. Cover yourself up in Muslim countries (this includes many parts of South-East Asia). Dress soberly, but smartly, in Japan and Korea.

■ **Modify your communication style to suit local expectations**
Many Asian cultures admire strong women and even elect them as their political leaders. But they dislike intensely the argumentative and assertive behaviour of some of the Western women they have to do business with.

Functional–personal

Everyone responds positively to genuine human warmth and empathy. Indeed, we believe it's at the heart of all successful business communication. If you're from a culture that falls to the left of this scale (for example, Germany, Switzerland, Scandinavia), however, you may not feel the need to build a close personal relationship with everyone you do business with. And you may feel surprised, or even impatient, if your business associates spend too much time on small talk or socializing. But, there are many cultures (for example, the Arab world, Asia, Southern Europe, Africa, South America) where people won't do business with you until they know and trust you. With them, you need to:

■ **Allow plenty of time.**
Don't expect to fly in, sign the contract and fly home on the same day. Be prepared to spend several meetings exchanging information about your two companies and the individuals involved before you start discussing specific business proposals.

■ **Engage in small talk.**
At the beginning of any meeting with someone from the Arab world, for example, it's not unusual to spend up to 45 minutes getting to know one another or cementing the relationship, and the conversation can extend to all aspects of life.

■ **Be prepared to socialize with your colleagues and clients.**
In countries as diverse as Spain and Japan, much important information is exchanged in a social context over a drink or a meal.

> ■ **Be prepared to exchange favours and small gifts.**
> Small favours, such as helping someone's son to find a school in
> your country, can do a lot to warm the relationship.

Physically distant–physically close

People from individualist cultures (like the United States, United
Kingdom, Northern Europe) tend to fall somewhere in the middle of this
scale. There are some group-oriented cultures (eg East and South-East
Asian) that fall to the far left of this scale and others (eg Arab, African,
Indian, Latin American, Southern Italian, Greek, Turkish) that fall to the
far right.

If you're doing business with someone from the middle of the scale:

> ■ **Give a firm, short handshake and look people in the eye.**
> If your handshake is too soft and your eye contact infrequent,
> they may conclude you're weak and untrustworthy.

When you're with people from the far left of the scale:

> ■ **Give them plenty of personal space.**
> If you touch them, stand too close, or look them too directly in
> the eye, you will make them feel very uncomfortable.

When your business associates are from the far right of the scale:

> ■ **Don't show surprise or embarrassment if they get too close.**
> In tactile cultures, handshakes can go on forever and you'll have
> almost no personal space. And it's often perfectly normal for
> men to kiss or hold hands with each other. Rejecting these signs
> of warmth will make you appear cold and discourteous.

Communication

Low context	High context								
Business relationships are complicated. Therefore, communication needs to be frank, explicit and direct.	Business relationships are complicated. Therefore, communication needs to be diplomatic, implicit and indirect.								
50 40 30 20 10	0 10 20 30 40 50								
Reserved	**Effusive**								
I think you should talk only when you have something relevant to say.	Lots of talk indicates warmth and interest. Silences should be avoided.								
50 40 30 20 10	0 10 20 30 40 50								
Written	**Spoken**								
For serious issues I prefer the written word.	For serious issues I prefer oral communication.								
50 40 30 20 10	0 10 20 30 40 50								

Low context–high context

Low context communicators tend to express themselves in explicit, concrete and unequivocal terms. There's little cultural baggage or 'context' attached to the words they use and you can usually assume that what they say is what they mean. The Americans, Scandinavians, Finns and Germans tend to fall at the far left of this scale. When you're doing business with them:

▪ **Take what they say literally.**
If they say something is *difficult,* they mean it's difficult – but not necessarily impossible.

▪ **Don't be offended if they openly contradict you or disagree.**
To them, stating the case clearly and unequivocally shows respect and honesty. They're not trying to be gratuitously insensitive or aggressive.

High context communicators, on the other hand, tend to communicate more implicitly. They expect you to be able to interpret what they mean from your knowledge of the cultural values that lie behind the words, what they're actually talking about at the time, their tone of voice and, of course, their eye and body language. People from China, Japan, the Arab world and France tend to be high context communicators. And the way the British use understatement, irony and allusion means that they too often lean towards the right of this scale. When you're doing business with high context communicators:

▨ **Don't always take what they say literally.**
If a Japanese colleague says something is *difficult*, he's probably telling you it's impossible. Look at his eye and body language and ask yourself how far it supports or detracts from the actual words he's using. Think too about the context and what you know about the situation. Wait. Listen. Ask gently.

▨ **Don't get suspicious or irritated if you find it hard to grasp their key message.**
Burying the key message in circular talk and allusion comes naturally to them. They're not doing it deliberately to confuse or mislead you. Be patient, listen hard, read between the lines, and ask questions to check you've understood them correctly.

Reserved–effusive

Your preferences on this scale will have a strong influence on how you instinctively play the conversation game. The Americans and British, for example, expect conversation to be relatively interactive. To them, interrupting with the odd relevant comment or question shows interest. The Japanese, Chinese, Scandinavians, Finns and Germans, on the other hand, are used to waiting their turn to speak. For them, conversation is often like a series of mini-monologues. When you're doing business with more reserved cultures:

▨ **Listen carefully to what they are saying without interrupting.**

▨ **Don't speak too effusively.**
You may think the whole world can be won over with a bit of charm and smooth talk. But very reserved cultures, such as the Finns, actively mistrust people who are too effusive.

And, unless they are German or Swiss:

▨ **Pause for a few seconds before giving your reply.**
The Scandinavians, Finns, Chinese and Japanese are usually very

comfortable with silence and will often pause after someone has spoken to show that they're thinking about what has been said.

If, on the other hand, your business partners are from a more effusive culture (for example, the Arab world, the United States, Italy, the United Kingdom):

■ **Don't be offended if they interrupt you.**
They're not being ill-mannered or disrespectful.

■ **Actively show interest in what they are saying.**
People who listen in total silence make them feel uncomfortable. So try to make the occasional comment: *I see* or *That surprises me* or *I didn't realize that.*

Written–spoken

Most Northern Europeans and North Americans would lean towards the left of this scale. For them, memoranda of understanding, written summaries and e-mailed offers may carry more weight than what people say in a meeting; and contracts almost certainly will. When you're doing business with them:

■ **Don't be offended if they take a lot of notes during the meeting.**
People from written cultures generally feel more comfortable relying on the written word rather than memory. If they take notes, it's not a signal that they don't trust you. They're just trying to be professional and get things right.

■ **Don't be surprised if they get their lawyers involved early on in the relationship.**
Again, it's not a signal that they don't trust you. They're just trying to make sure that everyone's interests are protected.

■ **Don't assume an agreement has been made until it has been confirmed in writing.**

For cultures (such as the Arab world) that have a strong oral tradition, on the other hand, the spoken word tends to be far more important. When you're trying to make deals with them:

■ **Don't take too many written notes during the meeting.**
If you do, they may think you don't trust them.

■ **Leave the lawyers at home.**
Oral cultures accept that contracts are a necessary part of an international deal; but they don't define or shape the relationship as they do in a more written culture. So don't bring the lawyers in until the whole deal has been agreed.

■ **Don't make oral promises you're not prepared to keep.**

Time

Monochronic						Polychronic				
I prefer to deal with one task at a time in a structured fashion.						I prefer to have several tasks running at the same time.				
50	40	30	20	10	0	10	20	30	40	50
Speed						Patience				
Too much analysis leads to paralysis.						Taking my time helps me make the right decision.				
50	40	30	20	10	0	10	20	30	40	50
Short-term						Long-term				
I prefer to focus on the here and now.						I need to see beyond the horizon and plan accordingly.				
50	40	30	20	10	0	10	20	30	40	50
Future						Past				
Tradition gets in the way of progress.						Change needs to respect tradition.				
50	40	30	20	10	0	10	20	30	40	50

Monochronic–polychronic

In monochronic cultures (for example, Anglo-Saxon America and Canada, Australia, Scandinavia, Germany, Switzerland, the Netherlands, the UK), time is linear, sequential, and can be cut up into blocks. People are judged by how well they can control their time. And those who can't do so are not to be trusted. The Germans and Swiss would probably fall at the far left of this scale. As they work out *Die Tagesordnung* (the Daily

Order), they will often allot a specific and precise amount of time to each task – including their coffee breaks. When dealing with such cultures, you would be wise to:

■ **Fix appointments weeks ahead.**
By doing so, you're communicating that the subject is important and that you are in control of your time.

■ **Send meeting agendas in advance.**
Or, at least, be ready to agree them at the beginning of meetings.

■ **Arrive on time.**
The Dutch and British are not as insistent on this as the Swiss, Scandinavians and Germans.

■ **Start meetings at the agreed time.**
If you keep visitors waiting outside your office, they'll assume you are disorganized and, therefore, not to be respected or trusted; or worse, they'll think you're deliberately trying to make them feel inferior. Many negotiations have been weakened from the start because of this kind of misinterpretation. If there's an unavoidable delay, explain the reason and apologize.

■ **Keep to agendas, schedules and deadlines.**
If you don't stick to the point, you'll be regarded as devious or unprepared.

■ **Interrupt if you don't understand something.**
If you wait until the end before admitting this, they will think of you as a time-waster.

■ **Give bad news straight away.**
If you don't, they may well conclude that you're being dishonest or deceitful.

Polychronic cultures (for example: Hispanic United States, Latin America, India, the Arab world, Italy) view time as more circular; it's their servant, not their master. To them, how you nurture relationships is more important than how you manage your time. When dealing with or in polychronic cultures, you should:

■ **Fix appointments at short notice.**
Don't be surprised if, even then, they have to be changed at the last moment.

■ **Allow plenty of time between appointments.**

◼ **Be prepared to be kept waiting.**
Use the time to chat to the receptionist, secretary or other visitors. You'll be surprised at how much useful information you can gather.

◼ **Try to fix an agenda at the start of a meeting.**
But don't stick to it rigidly. Allow the discussion to meander before gently trying to bring it back to the points you want to discuss. The way in which the other side meanders may well signal to you what points are important to them.

◼ **Avoid rushing meetings.**
Present your case in stages; ask and answer questions; use the many interruptions and parallel discussions to observe, think and plan.

◼ **Don't bind yourself to self-imposed deadlines.**
Follow the mood rather than the schedule. You will seriously undermine your negotiating position if you show you're desperate to meet quarterly targets or catch the plane home.

◼ **If there's bad news, try to soften it.**
You don't have to delay passing on the bad news for days or weeks. But try to spend some time at the beginning of the conversation preparing them for what you're going to say.

Speed–patience

You might expect all monochronic cultures to be keen to get everything done as fast and efficiently as possible; and all polychronic cultures to prefer taking their time. Unfortunately, life isn't that simple. Though the monochronic Germans often expect their meetings to be well structured and fairly quick, they can be very slow in taking decisions. With the more polychronic Spanish, on the other hand, meetings can be long and rambling, but decisions are often taken very rapidly. And the Japanese, who are well known for taking a very long time to actually reach a decision, expect implementation to be lightning-quick once a decision has been made.

The critical issue for the international negotiator is how fast you expect to progress from initial contact to final deal. And closely linked to that question is how much time you're prepared to devote to developing a personal relationship with your partners. If, like the Americans, you lean towards the far left of this scale, and you're trying to make a deal with partners who lean towards the right:

■ **Don't try to force the pace.**
If you do, your partners may well perceive you as pushy or arrogant. No matter how straightforward and attractive you think your offer is, focus on the relationship first, commercial issues second. Give your partners time to get to know you and discuss your proposals among themselves in a leisurely fashion.

And if, like the Mexicans, you lean to the far right of this scale, don't jump to any hasty conclusions about your prospective partners' motives. If the Mexicans in our case study had agreed to meet the Americans across the negotiating table, they would probably have liked them. And, who knows? The Americans might even have offered a better deal than the Swedes.

Short-term–long-term

In today's business world, shareholders of every culture put companies under pressure to show results in the short term. And even in Confucian cultures, like China, which are renowned for taking the long-term view, people are often quick to seize an opportunity for short-term personal gain.

Even so, there are some cultures that instinctively lean further to the right of this scale than others. While the Americans' impatience with time often leads them to insist on results in the short term, cultures as diverse as the Swiss and the Japanese tend to take a longer-term view. If you fall to the left of this scale and you're trying to manage a team who lean to the right, you should be careful not to jump to hasty conclusions. Reportees – like Connie the Swiss IT project manager – who take a longer-term view than you might like, are not necessarily lacking in dynamism or vision. Indeed, as Connie's American boss Robert found to his cost, their longer-term plan might turn out to be much more effective than your short-term one.

Future–past

The Americans (and other future-oriented cultures like the 'new Russia') tend to see tradition as one of the main barriers to progress. For people in much of the rest of the world, traditional values and the lessons of the past have a contribution to make to future development. China, Japan and India, for example, would fall to the far right of this scale, while many European countries would probably fall somewhere in the middle. While the futurists will be keen to introduce new systems, the traditionalists will be more interested in working out what went wrong with the old ones. If you place too much emphasis on the past, the former will think you're pessimistic, conservative and lacking in dynamism; if you focus exclusively on the future, the latter will perceive you as superficial.

So, when you're presenting to future-oriented cultures:

■ **Focus on the future, even if you're reporting on past results.**

And when you're presenting to people who value tradition:

■ **Include plenty of relevant background (ie past) detail even if you're making proposals for the future.**

Truth

Fixed						Relative				
There are clear rights and wrongs.						What is right and wrong depends on the circumstances.				
50	40	30	20	10	0	10	20	30	40	50
Analytical						Intuitive				
What I value most is a logical, comprehensive and consistent argument. Even if I instinctively feel a proposal is right, I need to test every step of the argument before I can commit myself.						What I value most are creative and intriguing ideas that appeal to the emotions. If I instinctively feel a proposal is right, I don't need to test every single step in the argument before I commit myself.				
50	40	30	20	10	0	10	20	30	40	50
Theoretical						Empirical				
I like using abstract concepts to solve problems.						For me, concrete experience is more important than theory.				
50	40	30	20	10	0	10	20	30	40	50

Fixed truth–relative truth

If you believe there are clear rights and wrongs regardless of the circumstances, you will probably expect people to follow rules and procedures to the letter. North Americans, Australians and northern Europeans lean this way. People from these cultures tend to attach great importance to written contracts, organization charts, detailed quality control manuals and so on. And they admire honesty and directness, even if it hurts people's feelings. When you're doing business with them, you should:

■ **Pay full attention to the written clauses of any contract you are negotiating.**
   In their eyes, you have committed to them – even if the situation changes. The language may look negative to you because it focuses on what to do if things go wrong; but the fixed truth culture sees it as no more than an insurance policy.

■ **Keep your bargaining range narrow.**
   People who move too far from their initial offer/proposal could be regarded as liars and cheats.

■ **Be prepared for open criticism or direct rejection of your proposals.**
   This may seem extremely rude to you; but people from fixed truth cultures often prefer to know where they stand. They won't pick up the correct messages if you're too vague and indirect. And they'll mistrust you if you keep them in the dark.

■ **Use arguments based on logic and the facts.**
   Avoid ones based on emotional appeals to family and friendship.

■ **Be very careful when giving presents or doing favours.**
   What you think of as simply a gift to strengthen the relationship, they may regard as a bribe.

In relative truth cultures (to be found in much of East, South-East and South Asia, Africa and around the Mediterranean), the circumstances dictate the way you behave. Your loyalty is more to your group (eg family, clan, friends and company) than to a set of abstract rules. When dealing with people from relative truth cultures, you need to:

■ **Focus on building the relationship before getting down to contractual details.**
   Keep your lawyers under control. Better still, leave them at home. The letter of intent may be considered more important than the contract.

■ **Keep your bargaining range wide.**
Relative truth cultures regard negotiating as a process to be enjoyed and a good opportunity to assess the other person's character. Too narrow a gap between opening offer and target makes it difficult for such judgements to be made.

■ **Be ready to renegotiate a contract if the situation changes.**

■ **Maintain continuity in relationships.**
The link is with the person, not the company. Any change of personnel needs careful handling. Give plenty of notice and make sure the *old hand* introduces his successor personally to your company's clients.

■ **Use emotional arguments which show the benefits to the person's group.**

■ **Avoid being too direct in your opinions.**
What may seem always right to you, may be completely *wrong at that moment* to them.

■ **Accept small gifts and favours.**
They are a sign of respect and friendship, not an attempt to corrupt you. Reciprocate by giving a present too; or if, for example, they have a relative or friend who plans to visit your country, offer to help them.

Analytical–intuitive

The French, Germans and Swiss would fall to the left of this scale. Their education has taught them to take a factual, balanced and above all logical view of any situation. If you want to get them on your side, make sure your argument is comprehensive and consistent. By all means be positive, but make sure you can support your enthusiasm with solid facts and rational argument. If you don't, they may well jump to the conclusion that you're superficial, or even lazy; and that what you're saying is meaningless hot air.

The Americans are impatient with time, willing to accept mistakes and happy to improvise. As a result, they would probably fall nearer the middle of this scale. The highly pragmatic British would lean towards the right. When you're dealing with more intuitive cultures, resist the temptation to give them too many facts. By all means construct a logical argument, but keep it short and to the point. If you don't, there's a danger they will think you are dull and unimaginative.

Theoretical–empirical

At first sight, you may think this scale is very similar to the previous one. But, actually, there are a number of logical cultures that prefer concrete experience to abstract theory. The Germans and Finns, for example, certainly favour logical argument, but they would fall to the right of this scale.

While the French also favour logical argument, they're more likely to base it on abstract concepts and would fall to the left of this scale.

The Americans, too, would probably lean to the left, which might be why they're more prepared than, for example, the Finns to commit themselves to aims and values that are expressed in relatively abstract terms.

For most Brits, concrete experience is more important than theory. So they're at the same time intuitive and empirical.

So before you can work out how best to argue your case, you need to think about where your international colleagues fall on both the analytical–intuitive and theoretical–empirical scales.

The meaning of life

Choice						Destiny				
I am in charge of how I live my life.						Forces beyond my control determine what happens in my life.				
50	40	30	20	10	0	10	20	30	40	50
Risk-embracing						Risk-averse				
I like taking risks.						I avoid taking risks.				
50	40	30	20	10	0	10	20	30	40	50

To many Westerners – even those who are regular churchgoers – religion is a private affair. It has little influence on their business lives. The meaning of life and death is for discussion in the university coffee bars and on late-night television. It comes as a shock to them when they find that many cultures have no such demarcation. In the Arab world, for example, religious and philosophical beliefs directly affect the way business is done.

When communicating in strongly and publicly religious cultures you must be careful to:

■ **Know and honour the local rules of behaviour.**

Many of them are based on religious practices. In Muslim and Hindu cultures, for example, eat and hand over documents with your right hand and don't show the soles of your feet. Don't offer alcohol or pork to Muslims. Be sensitive to the kosher food laws of orthodox Jews. In India and much of South-East Asia, accept that the contract will only be signed or the equipment installed on a day that is regarded as auspicious. Agree to have the site of your new factory blessed by Shinto priests in Japan and aligned correctly by the *feng shui* man in Southern China. Appreciate that the wrong doings in a previous life can explain your Indian employee's shortcomings in this one.

■ **Avoid blaspheming.**

Secular Europeans who casually swear (eg *God* or *Jesus Christ*) can cause great offence, not only to the many Americans, Africans and Asians (eg Koreans) who are strong Christians, but also to people of other religions. Some Muslim and Indian businessmen have told us that they would prefer to do business with a practising Christian than an overt atheist. How can you trust someone who has no beliefs?

■ **Assess attitudes to risk.**

In some cultures subordinates are encouraged to take risks and are rewarded for showing personal initiative. In others quite the opposite is the case and conformity is the norm. If you're managing a team from a risk-averse culture, you may need to be very patient and supportive if you want your staff to act in a more autonomous way.

Presentation style

Upbeat						Low-key				
I always try to emphasize the positive aspects of a situation. And I'm not afraid to talk openly about my own achievements and successes.						I always try to give a factual and balanced view of a situation. And if I've done a good job, I let the facts speak for themselves.				
50	40	30	20	10	0	10	20	30	40	50

Short						Long				
I keep my presentation short and to the point, never go over an agreed time limit, and speak as concisely as possible.						I allocate as much time to the subject as it deserves and try to speak as eloquently and impressively as possible.				
50	40	30	20	10	0	10	20	30	40	50

Selective						Comprehensive				
I select only the key points and avoid clouding my message with unnecessary detail.						I make sure my presentation is thorough and detailed with plenty of supporting facts and documentation.				
50	40	30	20	10	0	10	20	30	40	50

Persuade						Inform				
I state my own opinions and conclusions upfront and focus only on those areas that support my argument.						I give a detailed and balanced view of the whole situation, so that the audience can draw their own conclusions.				
50	40	30	20	10	0	10	20	30	40	50

Creative structure						Logical structure				
What I appreciate most is a creative structure that surprises and intrigues.						What I appreciate most is a well-structured, logical sequence of arguments.				
50	40	30	20	10	0	10	20	30	40	50

Upbeat–low-key

In the presentations we described to you, it was the Americans who were at the far left of this scale, and the Swiss and British who were at the far right. No one can expect the Americans to stop sounding enthusiastic and positive. Indeed, we believe that putting your message across persuasively and positively is something that all presenters should aim to do. So, by all means, be upbeat and enthusiastic. But if you're presenting to a low-key audience:

- Make sure you can support what you say with relevant details and facts.

- Respond to their concerns realistically and factually.

- Don't put too much emphasis on your own successes and achievements.

If, like Connie the Swiss woman or George the British fund manager, you come from a low-key culture and you are presenting to the Americans:

- Try to find an upbeat central message that looks forward rather than back.

- Make a conscious effort to *sound* positive and optimistic.

Short–long/selective–comprehensive

American and British audiences tend to respond best to presentations that are short and selective. When you're presenting to them:

- Be concise.

- Never go over an agreed time limit.

Italian, German, Scandinavian, Finnish and Japanese audiences fall to the right of these two scales. When you're presenting to them:

- Avoid being oversimplistic.

- Support your arguments with plenty of relevant facts and data.

Even if you're presenting to an audience who value a lot of facts and background information, however, it is still vital to be selective. Remember that the most dangerous subject for you as presenter is the one that fascinates you; the one that you're the world expert on.

Persuade–inform

The Americans, Italians and British would all fall to the left of this scale. They expect presenters to interpret the facts for them. When you're presenting to them:

- **Give them your opinions upfront and tell them directly what your recommendations are and why.**
- **Try to present your case as persuasively as possible.**

The Germans, Scandinavians, Finns and Japanese, on the other hand, expect you to let them draw their own conclusions. When you're presenting to them:

- **Avoid the hard sell.**

Creative structure–logical structure

The Germans, Scandinavians, Finns and French fall to the right of this scale; the Americans and British to the left. Try to adjust the way you present your argument accordingly. But remember that, no matter where your audience is from, they will only listen to what you say and remember the message you're trying to get across if you create a concrete context they can relate to. In this respect, we believe that all presenters need to demonstrate creativity. In our experience, the right metaphor will appeal to even the most logical of audiences. And finding that metaphor will often help you turn a satisfactory presentation into a brilliant one.

A final word

Our colleague, Richard, had been head of Canning's subsidiary in Japan for a few months. He had just come out of a meeting with an important client. He asked his Japanese sales manager how it had gone. *Very good* was the instant reply. Richard had been in the country long enough to know that this could mean the exact opposite. So he wasn't surprised when, after about two minutes, his sales manager said:

In Japan, we sometimes say that you have two eyes, two ears and one mouth.

It took a few seconds for Richard to realize that he had been severely criticized by his subordinate for speaking too much and observing too little. It was a very Japanese moment. But the saying is relevant to anyone doing business internationally.

It is the skilled observer who will adapt and win.

Appendix: False friends

At Canning, we have heard people using all of the false friends listed below. Often the misunderstandings caused have had humorous results; but sometimes, the consequences have been serious.

The lists are not comprehensive; nor do they include all cognates.

Section 1

The false friends in this section apply principally to speakers of Latin-based languages:

E = Spanish; F = French; I = Italian; P = Portuguese

However, some of them also apply to speakers of German and Nordic languages:

(D) = German; (N) = Norwegian; (S) = Swedish; (SF) = Finnish

Word	means this...	to speakers of these languages	but, to native speakers of English, it often means
account	Account Executive	I	facility for financial/commercial transactions – eg bank account
achieve	finish	F	reach, attain, acquire
action	company share	F	deed, act
actual	present, current	(D), E, F, I, P, (S)	real, existing in fact
actually	now, currently	(D), E, F, I, P	as a fact, really
advertise	warn	E	publicise
advise	warn	E	offer a recommendation/opinion
affluence	crowd	F	wealth, riches
agenda	diary	(D), E, F, I	a list of items for discussion
anxious	eager, greedy	E	worried
apparently	obviously	F	seemingly, it appears so
assist	attend, watch	E, F, P	help
attend	wait for, pay attention to	E, F	take part in, be present at
avocado	lawyer	E	a pear-shaped fruit
balance	balance sheet	I	equilibrium
benefit	profit	(D), E, F, I, P	advantage, helpful factor
candid	naive	F, P	frank, giving opinions openly
carpet	folder, file	E	floor covering
caution	security, guarantee	F	prudence, carefulness
chapter	heading	I	main division of a book
collaborator	colleague	F	one who cooperates with enemies
college	primary school	E	school for higher education
comfortable	convenient	F	giving ease
concurrence	competition	(D), F	simultaneous
conference	lecture, presentation	E	assembly, consultation, discussion
consistent	substantial, large	I	coherent, logical, unchanging
constipated	(have) a cold	E	find it hard to empty one's bowels
convenient	economical	I	helpful, opportune, accessible

Word	means this...	to speakers of these languages	but, to native speakers of English, it often means
delay	lead time	F	instance of being late
demand	ask for	F	insist on
direction	management	(D), F	line taken towards destination
educated	polite	E	well schooled
effective	real, actual	I	producing the desired result
engagement	commitment	F	appointment, betrothal
embarrassed	pregnant	E	self-conscious, uncomfortable
eventually	possibly, maybe	(D), E, F, I, (S)	finally
excuse	apology	F	reason given to justify fault
exercise	financial year	F	practice or training activity
exit	success	E	act of going out or leaving
expect	wait	I	regard as probable or appropriate
experience	experiment	F	knowledge or skill resulting from practice
figures	diagrams	F	numbers
formation	training	E, F, I, P	structure or arrangement
globally	generally	F	all over the world
holding	holding company	I	keeping possession of
idiom	language	E	group of words whose meaning has been established by usage
important	big	F	of high status or rank; high priority; significant
in case	if	F	in provision against a future event
incoherent	inconsistent	F	unintelligible, illogical
informal	irresponsible	E	without ceremony, unofficial
interesting	financially worthwhile	F	causing curiosity, holding the attention
issue	outcome	F	a point in question; a problem
large	long	E, I	big
mess	trade fair	(D), E, F, P, (S)	a state of disorder or confusion

Word	means this...	to speakers of these languages	but, to native speakers of English, it often means
morbid	soft	I	sickly, diseased, melancholy
notice	news	E	poster displaying public announcement; formal statement of future intention (eg to quit job)
of course!	sure!	F	obviously! (I'm not stupid)
parent	relative	E	mother or father
particular	private	E	individual
politics	policy	F	concerning the State or government
possibly	if possible	I	maybe, perhaps
preservative	condom	(D), E, F, I	substance for conserving perishable goods
presume	show off, boast	E	suppose to be true
pretend	assert, claim, require, intend, aspire	F E	claim falsely so as to deceive
problem	matter, question	I	difficult issue requiring a solution
prove	try, try on (clothing)	E	demonstrate the truth
realise	make real, implement, carry out	E, F	be aware or suddenly become aware
refer	report (to someone)	I	allude to
rentability	profitability	(D), F	the state of being rentable – suitable for renting
resume	summarise	E, F	start again after a break
safe	secure	F	free of danger or injury
safety	security	F	freedom from danger or risks
satisfactory	very good	F	adequate
scope	objective, aim, purpose	I	opportunity for action
sensible	sensitive	(D), E, F, I	having wisdom or common sense
signature	subject	E	name or initials used to sign a document

Word	means this...	to speakers of these languages	but, to native speakers of English, it often means
society	company	F, I	social community in which we live
suburb	slum	E	outlying districts of a city, usually residential
success	event	E	favourable outcome
surname	nickname	F	family name
sympathetic	nice, friendly	(D), E, F, I, P	able to share the emotion of others
terrific	terrifying, frightening	F, I	huge; excellent
topic	cliché	E	subject, theme
venue	time of meeting	F	meeting place

Section 2

The false friends in this list apply exclusively to speakers of German and Nordic languages:

D = German; N = Norwegian; S = Swedish; SF = Finnish

Word	means this...	to speakers of these languages	but, to native speakers of English, it often means
angina	tonsillitis	SF	pain in the chest
at last	lastly, finally	D	in the end after much delay
competent	well-qualified	D	capable, able
consequently	consistently	D, N, S	as a result
control	check	D	command, direct, restrain
great	big	D	grand, important, high status
hardly	hard	D	only just, only with difficulty
investigate	invest	D	examine, study carefully
meaning	opinion	D	significance, sense, interpretation
motorist	motorcyclist	SF	driver of a car
novel	short story	SF	full length work of fiction
oversee	overlook	D	supervise
prospect	brochure	D	future opportunity
protocol	minutes of meeting	D	rules of behaviour or etiquette; formal statement of a transaction
risky	strong	SF	potentially dangerous
shortly	briefly	D	soon

References

Books

Brannen, C and Wilen-Daugenti, T (1993) *Doing Business with Japanese Men: A Woman's Handbook*, Stone Bridge Press, California

Ehrmann, M (1927) *Desiderata*, quoted at http://www.geocities.com/Iswote/desiderata.html

Hall, E T and Reed Hall, M (1989) *Understanding Cultural Differences: Germans, French and Americans*, Intercultural Press, Yarmouth

Hammond, J and Morrison, J (1996) *The Stuff Americans are Made Of*, Macmillan, New York

Kielinger, T (1997) *Crossroads and Roundabouts*, Press and Information Office of the Federal Government, Bonn

Articles in periodicals

Castaignede, T (2003) *Rugby World*, February, IPC Media, London

Quotes

Carlyle, T (1843) *Past and Present*, quoted at http://www.cybernation.com/victory/quotations/subjects/quotes_responsibility.html

Dickinson, J (1768) *The Liberty Song*, quoted at http://americanhistory.si.edu/1942/campaign/campaign24.html

Kennedy, J F (20 January 1961) – inaugural speech, quoted at
www.yale.edu/lawweb/avalon/presiden/inaug/kennedy.htm

Kuhn, T (1970) *The Structure of Scientific Revolutions*, University of Chicago Press, Chicago

Michel de Montaigne (1533–1592), *Of the Useful and the Honorable, The Essays (Les Essais)*, bk. III, ch. 1, Abel Langelier, Paris (1588)

Pope, A (1688–1744), *Essay on Man*, Epistle ii, quoted at
http://poetryarchive.bravepages.com/NOPQ/pope.html and
http://www.bartleby.com/100/230.22.html

Russell, B (1928) *Sceptical Essays*, quoted at
http://www.positiveatheism.org/hist/quotes/russell.htm

Wien, B – quoted at
http://www.morganstanley.com/GEFdata/digests/20030207-fri.html#anchor3

William of Wykeham (1324–1404) Motto of Winchester College and New College, Oxford, quoted at
http://en2.wikipedia.org/wiki/williamofwykeham

Further reading

Culture in general

Adler, N and Gundersen, A (2007) *International Dimension of Organizational Behavior*, South Western Educational Publishing, Boston

Canning edited by Mattock, J (2004) *Cross-Cultural Communication: The essential guide to international business*, Kogan Page, London

Hall, E T (1959) *The Silent Language*, Doubleday, New York

Hall, E T (1976) *Beyond Culture*, Anchor Press/Doubleday, New York

Hoecklin, L (1994) *Managing Cultural Differences*, Addison-Wesley/EIU, Wokingham

Hofstede, G (1980) *Culture's Consequences*, McGraw-Hill, New York

Hofstede, G (1991) *Cultures and Organizations: Software of the mind*, McGraw-Hill, New York

Lewis, R D (1996) *When Cultures Collide*, Nicholas Brealey Publishing, London

Mattock, J (1999) *The Cross-Cultural Business Pocketbook*, Management Pocketbooks Ltd, Alresford, UK

Mole, J (1997) *Mind Your Manners*, Nicholas Brealey Publishing, London

Schneider, S C and Barsoux, J L (2002) *Managing Across Cultures*, Prentice Hall Europe, Hemel Hempstead

Trompenaars, F and Hampden-Turner, C (1997) *Riding the Waves of Culture: Understanding diversity in business*, McGraw-Hill, London

Specific cultures

The 'Culture Shock' series – published by Kuperard – provides useful general and business advice on a wide range of cultures. Below are a few of the other titles that we have found to be of particular interest:

Al-Omari, J (2003) *The Arab Way: How to work more effectively with Arab cultures*, How To Books, Oxford

Al-Omari, J (2003) *Simple Guide to the Arab Way: Practical tips on Arab culture*, Global Books Ltd, Folkestone

Hall, E T and Reed Hall, M (1989) *Understanding Cultural Differences: Germans, French and Americans*, Intercultural Press, Yarmouth

Hammond, J and Morrison, J (1996) *The Stuff Americans Are Made Of*, Macmillan, New York

Hampden-Turner, C and Trompenaars, F (1995) *The Seven Cultures of Capitalism: Value systems for creating wealth in the US, Britain, Japan, Germany, France, Sweden and the Netherlands*, Piatkus, London

Kielinger, T (1997) *Crossroads and Roundabouts*, Press and Information Office of the Federal Government, Bonn (also available from local German Embassies)

Presenting

Bowman, L (1999) *High Impact Presentations: A radical approach*, Bene Factum Publishing Ltd, Honiton, Devon, UK

Jay, R and Jay, A (1999) *Effective Presentation: How to create and deliver a winning presentation*, Financial Times Prentice Hall, Harlow

Mattock, J and Ehrenborg, J (1993) *Powerful Presentations*, Kogan Page, London

Negotiating

Acuff, F L (1997) *How to Negotiate Anything With Anyone, Anywhere Around the World*, Amacom, New York

Fisher, G (1982) *International Negotiations: A Cross-Cultural Perspective*, Intercultural Press Inc, Boston

Fisher, R, Ury, W and Patton, B (1997) *Getting to Yes*, Arrow, New York

Hendon, D W (1989) *How to Negotiate Worldwide*, Gower, Aldershot

Kennedy, G (1997) *Everything is Negotiable!*, Random House Business Books, New York

Ury, W (1991), *Getting Past No: Negotiating with difficult people*, Bantam Doubleday Dell, New York

WWW sites

Country details

BBC http://www.bbc.co.uk/news/1/hi/world/

CIA World Fact Book
http://www.cia.gov/cia/publications/factbook/index.html

Library of Congress Country Studies
http://lcweb2.loc.gov./frd/cs/cshome.html

Intercultural journals and research

Intercultural Communication Institute
http://www.intercultural.org/

Intercultural Press
http://www.interculturalpress.com/shop/index.html

Intercultural Relations.com
http://www.interculturalrelations.com/

International Academy for Intercultural Research
http://www.watervalley.net/users/academy/

International Journal of Cross-Cultural Management
http://www.sagepub.com/journal.aspx?pid=277

Canning articles and interviews

For a videoclip of Richard Pooley's interview with CNN, visit www.canning-itd.co.uk/tv.cfm. For articles by Richard Pooley and Chris Fox, visit www.canning-itd.co.uk/news/press/cfm.

Index

abstract–concrete scale *see* theoretical–empirical scale
accents, tuning in to   158
acquired status–given status scale   34–36, 56–60, 117, 163, 166–67
    negotiating examples   113, 121
acronyms   153
active versus passive sentences   105
African culture   164, 165, 166, 167, 168, 177
    see also Algerian culture; Botswana; South African culture
'African village' context example   100–01
age factors, given status cultures   35, 59, 117, 166
agendas   119–20, 173, 174
aggressive language   130
Algerian culture   125–26, 127, 130
Al-Omari, Dr Jehad   15, 68
American culture   164, 165, 177, 179
    acquired status   34, 35–36
    attitude to contracts   126
    communication style   74–75, 75–76, 169, 170, 171
    historical influences   89–90
    intuitive approach   9–14, 178
    language use   145–46
    mission statement example   6–7, 8
    monochronic approach   172–73
    negotiation style   111–13, 117, 118–19, 120, 123, 129, 130
    presentation style   87–89, 91, 94–95, 96, 175, 182, 183
    seven cultural forces   90
    social behaviour   72, 73, 78–79, 80, 81, 168
    stereotypical view of British   92

analytical–intuitive scale   11, 176, 178
appraisal system, given status example   34, 35–36
Arab culture   164, 165
    communication style   75, 170, 171
    given status   166
    negotiating style   117, 129, 167, 179
    social behaviour   68–69, 71, 73–74, 82, 168
    time and timing   15, 173–74
articles in periodicals   192
Asian cultures   164, 167, 177
    social behaviour   69–70
    see also Arab culture; Chinese culture; Indian culture; Japanese culture
'audience first' rule   86–87, 108
Australian culture   117, 172–73, 177
    flat hierarchy   26–27, 165
Austrian culture   89, 125–26
authority and power   21–44
    getting people to play ball   36–43
    handling hierarchies   23–30
    monitoring performance   32–36
    taking responsibility   30–32

Bannon, Gerard   139
bargaining range   133, 177, 178
beliefs and practices   45–64
    discretion versus dishonesty   60–63
    gifts, favours and bribes   52–56
    nepotism   56–60
    rules, regulations and laws of the land   47–52
    understanding others   125–28
blaspheming   180

body language   65, 82, 158–59
book references and further reading   191,
   193–95
Botswana, nepotism example   58–60
Brannen, Christalyn   115
bribes   52–56
British culture   164, 165, 168, 178, 179
   attitude to contracts   126
   communication style   41, 75–76, 77, 78,
      170, 171
   language use   145–46
   monochronic approach   172–73
   negotiating style   117, 129, 130
   presentation style   94–95, 96, 182, 183
   social behaviour   65–66, 67–68, 69, 71–72,
      73, 78–79
   stereotypical view of Americans   92–93
business entertainment   53–54

Canadian culture   172–73
Carlyle, Thomas   21
Castaignede, Thomas   65–66
central message, creating a   91–92, 108
central norms see party line interpretations
checking and clarifying   152
Chinese culture   165, 166, 175, 180
   negotiating style   117, 170
   nepotism example   2, 56–57
   rules example   49–52
choice–destiny scale   127, 179–80
choosing what to say   73–78
clarifying and checking   152
clarity of speech   157–58
closed questions   13, 43, 44
'coffee break' working rhythms examples
   14–16
colours, hidden dangers in   81–82
communication preference scales   17–20,
   74–78, 169–72
   see also low context–high context scale;
      reserved–effusive scale; written–spoken
      scale
communication techniques   150–59, 160
comprehensive–selective presentation scale   94,
   95, 181, 182
concrete–abstract scale see empirical–theoretical
   scale
concrete contexts for presentations   97–103,
   109
'conditional' approach   131–33
constitution change example, Australia   27
contexts for presentations   97–103, 109
contracts, role in negotiations   126–28, 177
conversation skills   71–73
corporate initiatives   8–14

'corporate seagulls'   14
corruption   53
creative structure–logical structure scale   97,
   181, 183
criticism   177
Crossroads and Roundabouts 96
cultural conditioning   4
cultural preference scales   2–3, 161–62
   see also under individual names of scales, eg
      acquired status–given status scale

dates, misunderstandings over   153
deal-making see negotiating skills
decision-making differences   32
Desiderata   46
destiny–choice scale   127, 179–80
Dickinson, John   5
discretion/dishonesty limits   60–63
Doing Business with Japanese Men   115
'donations' example   54
double checking   152–54
dress for women   167
'drunk sales manager' example   45–46
Dutch culture   164, 165
   attitude to contracts   126
   monochronic approach   172–73
   negotiating skills   116–17, 128
   'truth telling' example   60–62

East Africa, presents example   54–55
effusive–reserved scale   73, 169, 170–71
Ehrmann, Max   46
empathy   38–41, 43
empirical–theoretical scale   7–8, 176, 179
English culture see British culture
English language   75, 104–07, 132–33,
   137–60
   British/American usage   145–46
   communication techniques   150–59
   false friends   143–45, 185–90
   idioms and phrases   146–49
   verbs and nouns   140–43
European culture, responsibility example
   31–32
exploratory approach to negotiating   133–34
eye contact   69–70, 168

false friends   143–45, 185–90
   German and Nordic examples   190
   Latin-based examples   185–89
family loyalties see nepotism
favours   52–56, 168, 177, 178
female relatives, questions about   82
financial control–profit centre differences
   41–43

Finnish culture   165, 179
  communication style   74–75, 169, 170
  negotiating style   122
  presentation style   182, 183
  social behaviour   71, 72, 73
fixed truth–relative truth scale   47–48, 122,
  133, 176, 177–78
flat hierarchy–vertical hierarchy scale   16,
  23–29, 163, 165–66
'football' presentation context example
  98–99
formal settings for negotiations   121
French culture   164, 178, 179
  attitude to contracts   126
  communication style   17–19, 75, 170
  corporate initiative case   9–14
  false friend examples   143–44
  gift giving examples   54, 55
  hierarchy example   23–24
  language use   152–53
  negotiating style   36–40, 121–22
  performance monitoring example   33
  presentation style   96–97, 183
  social behaviour   65–66, 67–68, 74, 80, 82
functional–personal scale   53, 131, 164,
  167–68
future–past scale   120, 172, 175–76

generalizations   3
German culture   165, 167, 178, 179
  communication style   74–75, 78, 169, 170
  false friend examples   144–45, 190
  language use   153–54
  monochronic approach   15, 172–73
  negotiating style   115–16, 117, 129, 130,
  174
  performance monitoring examples   33
  presentation style   96, 182, 183
  rules example   49–52
  social behaviour   67–68, 69, 71–72, 73, 74,
  80
Germanic-based English words   106–07, 141
gestures   81–82
'getting people to play ball'   36–43
gift-giving seasons, Japan   53
gifts   52–56, 168, 177, 178
given status–acquired status scale   34–36,
  56–60, 117, 163, 166–67
  negotiating examples   113, 121
Greek culture   168
greeting people   65–66, 67–70
group-oriented–individualist scale   29–30,
  30–32, 70, 163, 164
  negotiating examples   117, 122
guanxi   51

Hall, Edward T   12, 18
Hammond, J   90
handshaking   65–68, 69, 70, 168
'hidden dangers'   81–82
hierarchies   16, 21–30, 163, 165–66
high context–low context scale   18–19, 74–77,
  129, 169–70
'high level proposal' language example
  145–46
Hindu religious beliefs   180
Howard, John   27
HQ–subsidiary cases
  communication styles   17–19
  performance monitoring   34
  working rhythms   14–16
human element in speaking   158
humour   78–81

idioms   149
immoral–illegal dilemmas   49
impact, speaking with   103–07, 109
Indian culture   165, 166, 168, 180
  negotiation style   117, 175
  polychronic culture   173–74
  vertical hierarchy example   25, 27–28
individualist–group-oriented scale   29–30,
  30–32, 70, 163, 164
  negotiating examples   117, 122
Indonesian 'donation' example   54
inform–persuade scale   96, 181, 183
Inshillah   127
insulting language   130
interpreters   114
interrupting   151–52
intuitive–analytical scale   11, 176, 178
Irish 'working rhythm' example   14–16,
  19
irony   78–79
Italian culture   164, 165, 166, 168
  attitude to contracts   126
  communication style   41, 171
  false friend example   145
  negotiation style   129
  polychronic approach   173–74
  presentation style   95, 96, 182, 183
  rules example   47–49
  social behaviour   67–68, 69, 82

Jante Law   26
Japanese culture   164, 166, 175, 180
  communication style   17–19, 36–40, 75,
  183–84, 170
  gift exchange   53, 55
  hierarchy examples   23–24, 29–30
  language use   152–53, 153

negotiating styles 115, 116–17, 121–22, 128, 129, 174
  presentation style 182, 183
  responsibility example 31–32
  social behaviour 69–70, 71, 72, 80, 81
  'withholding the truth' example 60–62
Jewish religious beliefs 180
'joint' false friend example 143–44
jokiness 79–81

Kennedy, John F 111
Kielinger, Thomas 78, 96
kindness, small acts of 55
kissing 68, 69
'knowing the form' see social behaviour
'knowing the limits' see beliefs and practices
'knowing your place' see authority and power
'knowing yourself' 161–84
  communication 169–72
  meaning of life 179–80
  presentation style 181–83
  relationships 163–68
  time 172–76
  truth 176–79
Kuhn, Thomas 85

language 129–34
  see also English language
Latin American culture 165, 168
  negotiation style 117, 120
  polychronic culture 173–74
  see also Mexican culture
Latin-based English words 106–07, 141
Latin-based languages, false friend examples 185–89
laws of the land, obeying 47–52
lawyers in negotiations 113–14, 171, 177
leadership, different definitions of 32
letters, misunderstanding over 152–53
'lion-tamer' presentation example 103
listening, importance of 12, 20, 43
location of negotiations 118, 120–23, 135
logical structure–creative structure scale 97, 181, 183
long–short presentation scale 94, 95, 181, 182
long-term–short-term scale 89, 172, 175
low context–high context scale 18–19, 74–77, 129, 169–70
low-key–upbeat scale 89–92, 181, 182

majalis (madeef, madafa, diwanihey) 74
'Management by Objectives' language example 155–56
manners see social behaviour
maps, use in presentations 101–03

'mathematics teaching' context example 100–01
'meaning of life' preference scales 179–80
  see also choice–destiny scale; risk-embracing–risk averse scale
Mercator's v Peters' world maps 102
Mexican culture, negotiating example 111–13, 119, 121, 123, 134–36, 175
mian zi 51
Middle East destiny cultures 127
mission statements, attitudes to 6–8
monochronic–polychronic scale 15, 118, 119, 172–74
moral values see beliefs and practices
Morrison, J 90
Muslim religious beliefs 180
'must' 147–48

native v non-native speakers 137–38, 139
negotiation styles 3, 111–36
  further reading 194–95
  pace and place 118–23
  picking the right people 113–18
  playing the game to win 123–34
nemawashi 32, 117, 122
nepotism 56–60
'newspaper' presentation example 99–100
non-native v native speakers 137–38, 139
Nordic languages, false friend examples 190
North American culture 171, 177
  see also American culture; Canadian culture
Northern European culture 53, 168, 171, 177
  mission statement example 6–7, 8
  social behaviour 74, 82
  see also under cultures of individual countries, eg British culture
Norwegian culture, use of humour 79–80, 81
note-taking 171
nouns 104, 140–41
numbers
  hidden dangers 81–82
  misunderstandings over 153

'objectives' language example 155–56
observing, importance of 151
o-chugen gift-giving season 53
'Offshore English' (OE) 3, 4, 138, 150–51, 158
'offstage' negotiations 121
'OK' 148–49
open questions 13, 42–43, 44
organization charts 21–22
o-seibo gift-giving season 53
'over the moon' idiom example 149

pace of negotiating 118–20, 135
party line interpretations 5–20
  communication styles 17–20
  corporate initiatives 8–14
  mission statements 6–8
  working rhythms 14–16
passive versus active sentences 105
past–future scale 120, 172, 175–76
paternalistic attitudes 35, 166
patience–speed scale 118–19, 172, 174–75
pausing during speaking 157
people, picking the right 113–18, 135
performance monitoring 32–36
personal connections, China 50–51
personal–functional scale 53, 131, 164,
  167–68
personal questions, asking 82
personal relationships, importance of 113,
  123, 131
personal space 68–69, 168
persuade–inform scale 96, 181, 183
Peters' v Mercator's world maps 102
phrasal verbs 141–43
physically distant–physically close scale
  68–69, 168
place of negotiations 118, 120–23, 135
'playing the game to win' 123–34, 136
'please' 146–47
Poland, hierarchy example 28
polychronic–monochronic scale 15, 118, 119,
  172–74
Pooley, Richard 25
Pope, Alexander 161
positive approach to negotiating 133–34
power see authority and power
preference scales 2–3, 161–62
  see also under individual names of scales, eg
    acquired status–given status scale
present tense 132–33
presentation skills 3, 85–109
  context 97–103
  further reading 194
  impact 103–07
  style 87–97
presentation style preference scales 181–83
  see also creative structure–logical structure
    scale; persuade–inform scale;
    selective–comprehensive scale; short–long
    scale; upbeat–low-key scale
'Prisoners' Dilemma' game 123–24
professional group culture differences 41–42
profit centre–financial control differences
  41–43
'provisions' false friend example 144–45
'pushing the right buttons' 12

'quality chart' example 9–14
quotations 192

regulations 47–52
rejection 177
relationship preference scales 163–68
  see also flat hierarchy–vertical hierarchy scale;
    functional–personal scale;
    individualist–group-oriented scale;
    physically distant–physically close scale
relative truth–fixed truth scale 47–48, 122,
  133, 176, 177–78
religious practices 179–80
Renault-Nissan Alliance 23–24, 115
reserved–effusive scale 73, 169, 170–71
respect 166
responsibility, attitudes towards 30–32
'reworking the figures' example 45
rhetoric (Rhetorik) 95, 96
rhythms of work 14–16, 172–74
risk-embracing–risk-averse scale 129–30,
  179–80
rituals 82
Romance-based words see Latin-based English
  words
Romania, withholding the truth example 62
rule bending 47–52
Russell, Bertrand 45
Russian culture
  discretion example 62–63
  performance monitoring example 33

Sandemose, Aksel 26
Saudi Arabian culture 73–74
scales, cultural preference 2–3, 161–62
  see also under individual names of scales, eg
    acquired status–given status scale
Scandinavian cultures
  communication styles 74–75, 170
  flat hierarchy examples 25–26, 165
  functional approach 167
  low context communication 169
  monochronic culture 172–73
  presentation style 182, 183
  social behaviour 71, 80
  see also Finnish culture; Norwegian culture;
    Swedish culture
selective–comprehensive presentation scale 94,
  95, 181, 182
sentences 104, 105, 154
'sharing information' ethos 63
sharp practice 53
Shaw, George Bernard 75
short–long presentation scale 94, 95, 181, 182
short-term–long-term scale 89, 172, 175

signposting 156
silence in conversations 72, 171
small acts of kindness 55
small talk 70–71, 119, 167
social behaviour 65–83
    avoiding hidden dangers 81–82
    conversation 71–73
    greeting 67–70
    humour 78–81
    small talk 70–71
    what to say and how 73–78
social code, Scandinavia 26
socializing 167–68
SOPHOP (soft on people, hard on points)
        approach 131
South African culture 29–30
South American culture 166, 167
South-East Asian culture 165, 168
Spanish culture 165, 174
    beliefs and practices 62–63
    false friend example 145
    given status 34, 35–36, 166
speaking skills
    clarity 157–58
    impact 103–07, 109
speed control, speaking 157
speed–patience scale 118–19, 172, 174–75
spoken–written scale 125–26, 169, 171–72
Steel Authority of India 27–28
stereotypes, reinforcing negative 92–93
Stuff Americans Are Made Of, The 90
styles of presentation 87–97, 108–09
subconscious mind, overcoming own 66
subsidiary–HQ examples
    communication styles 17–19
    performance monitoring 34
    working rhythms 14–16
'sugar the pill' example 19
summarizing 107, 127, 156
Swedish culture
    flat hierarchy 25–26
    negotiating style 112, 134–36
    nepotism example 2, 56–57
    world map example 102–03
Swiss culture 178
    functional approach 167
    hierarchy type 165
    monochronic approach 14–16, 19, 172–73

presentation style 87–89, 90–91, 175, 182
rules example 47–49
social behaviour 67–68, 71, 73
symbols 81–82
synonyms 155–56

Tall Poppy Syndrome 26–27
team choice 113–15
tempo control in presentations 107
'thank you', ways of saying 73–74
theoretical–empirical scale 7–8, 176, 179
time/timing preference scales
        172–76
    see also future–past scale;
        monochronic–polychronic scale; short-
        term–long-term scale; speed–patience scale
times, misunderstandings over 153–54
tone control in presentations 107
touching 68–69
translation pitfalls 74
    see also false friends
truth preference scales 176–79
    see also analytical–intuitive scale; fixed
        truth–relative truth scale;
        theoretical–empirical scale
Turkish culture 69, 168

UK see British culture
Understanding Cultural Differences 12
upbeat–low-key scale 89–92, 181, 182
USA see American culture

verbs 104–05, 140–43
vertical hierarchy–flat hierarchy scale 23–29,
        163, 165–66
volume control (speaking) 157–58

Walker, Gary 72
websites 192, 195
Wien, Byron 120
Wilen, Tracey 115
William of Wykeham 65
women, role of 114–15, 167
working rhythms 14–16, 172–74
world maps, differences in 102–03
written–spoken scale 125–26, 169, 171–72

zhou houmen 51